THE BASEBALL GODS ARE REAL
Volume 2: The Road to the Show

The BASEBALL GODS *are* REAL

Vol. 2: THE ROAD *to* THE SHOW

JONATHAN A. FINK

The Baseball Gods are Real
Volume 2: The Road to the Show

Written by Jonathan A. Fink
Copyright 2019

Polo Grounds Publishing LLC

Credit and thank you to Meg Reid for Book Cover Design and Book Layout.

Credit and thank you to Meg Shader for Editing.

Credit and thank you to Abi Laksono for Polo Grounds Publishing Logo.

Credit and thank you to Kim Watson for my Biography Picture.

Thank you to my Mom and Dad, Beth and Jeffrey Fink, for their help, guidance and support.

And thank you to my wife, Reggie, and my kids, Kayla and Nate, for their patience, understanding and support.

This book is dedicated to Martin Koslow
(March 24, 1920 – January 20, 2019)

The Husband, The Father, The Grandfather,
The Great Grandfather, The Gardener, The Dog Walker,
The Investor, The Stamp Collector, The Music Lover

TABLE OF CONTENTS

Dear Karen,

May the Baseball Gods and the Investment Gods always be with you!

Namaste,

Jonathan Fink

INTRODUCTION

"The baseball gods are showing me a little bit of everything this year. We just seem to make a mistake at the most inappropriate time."
—Willie Randolph

MY DEBUT BOOK, *THE BASEBALL GODS ARE REAL: A TRUE Story About Baseball and Spirituality,* chronicled the first part of my life, from elementary school through college, and described some of my earliest professional career experiences. It also recounted my midlife crisis at age thirty-eight, which inspired me to explore a spiritual path, and described how I transformed myself through a practice of yoga and meditation. During this transformative process, I was introduced to "the Baseball Gods," a term used to explain the mysterious and coincidental events that occur in the world of baseball. When baseball fans, players, managers, coaches, sports broadcasters and sports writers witness these miracle moments, they often refer to this mystical force in the universe as the work of the Baseball Gods.

Traversing through childhood, college, the music industry, Wall Street and, of course, the world of baseball, my first book took readers along for the ride as I experienced many synchronicities, winks from the universe, and divine guidance. In this book, *The Baseball Gods are Real – Volume 2: The Road to the Show*, I chronicle the next chapter of my life as I continue on my spiritual path.

The Road to the Show also follows the professional baseball career of Jon Perrin, my Satya Investment Management colleague, as he travels through the minor leagues on his road to the major leagues, known as "the show." I met Perrin during the baseball offseason of 2016, when he was working three jobs to makes ends meet. A chance encounter at Zoë's Kitchen, a restaurant near my hometown of Leawood, Kansas, led to a friendship that eventually blossomed into his apprenticeship and employment as a professional registered investment advisor with Satya. As Perrin's new investment advisory career begins, his struggle to get to the show continues.

Like Perrin, I continue on my path taking my readers with me all across America, from Arizona to Florida, from Wisconsin to California, from Colorado to Arkansas, from Mississippi to Iowa, and share my experiences as an author and die-hard baseball fan. I showcase many interesting baseball personalities I met along the way and tell stories about a few baseball legends, famous and not-so-famous ballparks I visited, and great baseball movies I have seen. This book also describes the fun I had promoting my first book with a book signing, a book club meeting, podcast interviews, and the use of a guerilla marketing strategy.

I truly enjoyed writing *The Baseball Gods are Real – Volume 2: The Road to the Show*. It was a labor of love. I hope my readers enjoy the ride as much as I did.

CHAPTER ONE

The Phoenix

"And once the storm is over, you won't remember how you made it through, how you managed to survive. You won't even be sure whether the storm is really over. But one thing is certain. When you come out of the storm, you won't be the same person who walked in. That's what this storm's all about."

—Haruki Murakami

THE BASEBALL GODS DEFINITELY PLAYED A ROLE IN introducing Jon Perrin to me and setting the stage for things to come. How else can you explain the way our paths crossed? I was having lunch at Zoë's Kitchen, a neighborhood restaurant on 135th Street in Overland Park, Kansas, when this guy who worked behind the counter came up to ask me about the financial reports I was reading. I quickly learned that, just like me, Perrin loved sports, geopolitics and investing, so the two of us became acquaintances and, over time, friends.

After two months of getting to know each other, Perrin and I met for a cup a coffee. That's when he very casually told me he was a professional baseball player, a pitcher. I was very surprised to hear this, as I suspect any avid baseball fan would be. Our initial encounter led us to become good friends and, ultimately, colleagues.

Planning for his future beyond baseball, for several months Perrin studied hard to learn as much as he could about financial planning and the stock market. Being fully prepared, he passed the exam to become a registered investment advisor. However, baseball was in his blood and in January 2017, after having passed the exam, Perrin told me he was invited to join the Milwaukee Brewers major league club in Arizona for spring training. Perrin was about to get his first glimpse of "the show."

After spending the fall and winter months of 2017 working closely with Perrin and getting to know him well, I was determined to visit his first major league spring training camp and attend his first game in person. As I have come to expect, the Baseball Gods were already way ahead of me making plans. I was pleasantly surprised to learn that on opening day of the Arizona Cactus League, the Brewers had "split squad" games on their schedule. For those unfamiliar with spring training rituals, split squad games occur when half the players on a team play a home game while the other half of the players travel to play a game at another team's stadium. It turned out that the Brewers were scheduled to play the Chicago Cubs at home at their Maryvale, Arizona, spring training facility and simultaneously play an away game at the San Francisco Giants' stadium in Scottsdale. Since the Brewers would need to field two teams at the same time, they would need extra players, especially pitchers.

As I was packing the car to leave for the airport, I received a text from Perrin saying that he was on the docket to pitch the next day on the road against the Giants in the second inning. I was thrilled to have him confirm that I would definitely see him pitch the next day in sunny Arizona.

I arrived at Kansas City International Airport, checked in for my flight to Phoenix, and sat down in the crowded waiting area near my gate. A man sitting across from me looked vaguely familiar and I could tell that he was struggling to recall who I was as well. As I settled into my seat, took out my headphones and a book to read, I noticed the man was still staring at me, hoping to put a name to my face. This staring contest continued for a few more minutes, until I decided to declare a truce and introduce myself before this awkward situation went into round two.

I approached the man and got a closer look at his somewhat familiar face, and then it hit me. He was Benny Harding, the father of Robin Harding, one of my wife Reggie's childhood friends. As we shook hands, I remembered seeing Benny at the Jewish Community Center (JCC) in Overland Park a few years before when he gave a passionate speech on Holocaust Remembrance Day. Benny's speech that day was particularly emotional for me. He, like my father-in-law, Sam Devinki, was born in Europe shortly after the end of World War II into a Jewish family that had experienced and survived the horrors and atrocities of the Holocaust, one of the darkest times in world history.

I mentioned to Benny that I was Jonathan Fink, Sam Devinki's son-in-law. When he heard the name "Devinki," his face lit up like a menorah on the last night of Chanukah. Clearly, there was a special place in Benny's heart for the Devinki family, especially Reggie's grandparents, Maria and

Fred Devinki, who, like the Harding family, had left Europe and settled in Kansas City, their promised land.

The ensuing conversation with Benny revealed that during the Holocaust his father was moved around to eight different concentration camps and his mother, who was just twelve years old at the time, also was moved several times from one concentration camp to another. After the war, Benny's family was relocated into a camp for displaced persons, and that's where Benny was born. Just like my father-in-law, Sam, Benny was only three years old when he and his parents arrived in Kansas City to start a new life in America.

I asked Benny why he was flying to Phoenix. He said that he and his wife had a home in Arizona, which they had purchased as a retreat to escape the harsh winters of Kansas City, and he was traveling to meet up with her. When asked, I told Benny that I was traveling to Phoenix to visit my apprentice, Jon Perrin, who was in Arizona for spring training with the Milwaukee Brewers. Then I told Benny the story about how I met Perrin, how we became friends, and how we eventually became colleagues.

Before too long, I was also telling Benny all about my first Baseball Gods book, which I had just finished writing. At one point, I mentioned the chapter in the book that described our recent Devinki family pilgrimage to Wodzislaw, Maria and Fred's hometown in Poland. There we visited the hole in the ground in the barn on the farm where the Devinki family hid from the Nazis for twenty-seven months during the Holocaust. Benny became emotional and was almost brought to tears as I was telling him this story.

After a pause to ease our emotions, I also told Benny how

Maria's wedding gift to Reggie and me changed the course of my professional asset management career. Bubbi Maria gave us our first gold coin as a gift on our wedding day, and I have been a proud "gold bug" ever since.

At that moment Benny pulled something out of his pocket. It was his money clip, but it wasn't just an ordinary money clip by any means. Benny's cash was held tightly together by a gold-plated money clip and on its top was an authentic American Eagle .999 gold bullion coin. Looking at me, Benny said he never left home without it. Then our eyes shifted back to Benny's gold coin money clip and we both stared at it for a moment. No additional words were needed. Our eyes made contact again and both of us smiled in recognition of its significance.

Benny and I agreed that meeting each other that morning at the Kansas City airport to board the same nonstop flight to Phoenix was not a coincidence. Our emotional bond had been codified. We hugged, said goodbye, and boarded the aircraft. Then, before falling asleep on the plane as I usually do, I thought about Benny's emotional speech years ago at the JCC and why I was there to hear it.

I awoke to the pilot's announcement that we were thirty minutes away from landing at the Phoenix Sky Harbor International Airport in Arizona. I thought about how important and symbolic this upcoming trip was going to be for me. It was a temporal marker in my life and I knew it. I was on my way to see Jon Perrin pitch in his first "big league" game. Having recently founded my own investment firm, Satya Investment Management, after devoting thirteen years to Morgan Stanley working as a financial advisor, I was also on my way to officially sign my apprentice as Satya's first employee. Placed neatly in my backpack was a Satya employment agreement with an "x" marking the spot where Perrin would sign his name.

Also with me in my backpack was the final draft of my first book, *The Baseball Gods are Real.* Reminding myself to always be a humble yogi, I realized at that moment how far I had come on my spiritual path. At the same time, I realized how far I had yet to go.

After the wheels of the plane touched down, we taxied on the tarmac to our gate. On route, I pondered the symbolism of the name of this city, Phoenix. In Greek mythology, the phoenix is a long-lived bird that cyclically regenerates and is continuously born again. Associated with the sun, a phoenix obtains new life by rising from the ashes of its predecessor. According to some sources, the phoenix dies in a show of flames and combustion. Looking back on my Wall Street years and ahead to the Satya years, I could easily relate to the Greek legend of the phoenix. I, too, felt like my old self had died and my soul had been born again.

CHAPTER TWO

The Cactus League

"I'd rather be optimistic and wrong than pessimistic and right."
—Elon Musk

AFTER LEAVING SKY HARBOR INTERNATIONAL AIRPORT in my Enterprise rental car, I checked in at my hotel and then headed straight to Jon Perrin's Spring training apartment in Glendale, Arizona. On my drive I was reminded of a rental car experience during my first trip to spring training in 2017, a memorable father-son adventure with my son, Nate. The car that I had reserved was not available when we checked in, so the desk manager gave us an upgrade to a Ford Mustang convertible. As we drove all around Arizona in a Mustang convertible, I had no doubt the Baseball Gods had something to do with it.

Perrin's apartment was easy to find because it was located right across the street from the Arizona Cardinals' football stadium. Before making plans to go out for dinner, I took a copy of the draft of my first book out of my backpack and gave it to Perrin for him to read when he had the chance.

Next, I pulled out Perrin's Satya employment agreement for him to review. Perrin had signed his first professional baseball contract when he was drafted by the Milwaukee Brewers after his senior year of college and now he was signing the first contract of his professional business career. After Perrin read, reviewed and signed the agreement, we shook hands and I said to him with considerable pride, "Congratulations, welcome to Satya!"

At dinner I asked Perrin about his first few weeks in major league spring training camp. Perrin smiled as he began to describe his Brewers clubhouse experience. He compared Brewers spring training to being in baseball heaven. Since I knew Perrin loved to eat, I asked him about major league food. Perrin laughed and said there clearly was a huge difference between the meals you get in the major league versus the minor league. He compared the food in the minors to eating at a fast food joint or at a one-star hotel, while the food served in the majors was like eating at a fine restaurant or at the Four Seasons Hotel.

This conversation with Perrin reminded me of a time in my life when I, too, was frequenting fast food joints because my resources were limited. Upon graduating from Tulane in 1996, I came home to New York to live with my parents in Armonk in Westchester County. After a few weeks, it became clear that I needed my own space. My folks were going to bed for the evening at the same time I was going out for the night, and they were getting up in the morning to go to work as I was coming in the door from my night out scouting bands. So, I moved into Manhattan and shared a small apartment on West 74th Street with one of my best friends, Eric Milano.

We shared one bathroom and my bedroom measured six by eight. Even the six-by-nine area rug my parents bought for me was too big for the room. At that time, many of my meals consisted of two hot dogs, with mustard and sauerkraut piled high, and a soda, known as the "dollar special" at Gray's Papaya located on Broadway and 71st Street on Manhattan's Upper West Side. Another of my meal choices back then was a dozen hot and spicy chicken wings for $1.99, at the bar only, at Malachy's Donegal Inn on 72nd Street between Columbus and Amsterdam Avenues. I might as well have been in the minor leagues eating my meals with Perrin. Hard to believe I'm a vegetarian now, bordering on vegan.

Contrasting his days in minor league training camps, Perrin explained that everything at the major league spring training facility was top notch. Then he went on to describe his locker room experience. The players would stroll into the clubhouse first thing in the morning and head to their lockers, which were always cleaned out overnight and reorganized prior to the players' arrival. Everything was folded perfectly and spotlessly clean. The lockers were also much larger than those Perrin was used to in the minors. He added that the locker room staff couldn't be more helpful. Attention to every detail was the norm. And the food was delicious and plentiful. In his view, it was just perfect. The smile on Perrin's face as he provided these details showed not only his gratitude, but also his appreciation for how far he had traveled on his road to the show.

This conversation with Perrin made me think about how many others have gone through a similar experience in their chosen profession. Think about actors, like Leonardo

DiCaprio, who start out doing TV commercials and playing bit parts and ultimately go on to win an Academy Award. Or a rock band, like Phish, that starts out playing fraternity houses and small clubs near a college campus and years later goes on to play 17 straight sold out performances at Madison Square Garden, perhaps the most well-known sports and music venue in the world. Or an investment professional who starts out in a small, windowless cubical and ends up in a large office, with floor to ceiling windows, overlooking the Statue of Liberty in New York City harbor. In some way, I could relate to Perrin's comparison of his minor league to major league experience.

My conversation with Perrin shifted from his locker room situation to his on-field experiences. I asked him if he had participated in any live pitching sessions yet. It turns out that the first batter Perrin faced in live batting practice was former Kansas City Royal and World Series champion Lorenzo Cain.

Cain had recently signed a long-term contract with the Brewers, the team he had started his career with as a rookie. Perrin described each pitch he had thrown to Cain in detail. It was amazing to me that Perrin could still remember every pitch he threw to Cain, even though it happened several weeks before. It was like a professional golfer being interviewed on television remembering every one of his 68 shots on the golf course that day. Perrin and Cain had a nice duel that day which Perrin ultimately won when Cain weakly grounded out to second base. Pleased, I said to Perrin, "You got Lorenzo Cain out. Amazing, just amazing!"

Perrin mentioned that a few days later, after a long practice, he found himself in the hot tub area with Cain. He told Cain how incredible it was for him, as a big fan and local kid from Olathe, Kansas, to see the parade in downtown Kansas City honoring the Royals after they won the 2015 World Series Championship. Watching him talk about pitching to and later chatting with a World Series hero like Lorenzo Cain, I could see that Perrin was in awe and truly embracing his time in baseball heaven.

Perrin then told me of another awe-inspiring moment during his spring training time with the big-league club, his interesting encounter with Brewers superstar outfielder Ryan Braun. One day during training camp, Braun approached Perrin and said that he heard from pitcher Brent Suter that Perrin had earned his Series 65 investment license in the offseason and was now a professional registered investment advisor. Braun, a personal investor himself, enjoyed following the ups and downs of the stock market and inner workings of Wall Street and was excited to have a teammate with whom he could discuss these subjects. I learned that Braun and Perrin spoke for about an hour discussing stocks, capital markets, the global economy, and other related topics. Here was Jon Perrin, at major league spring training camp, talking stocks on a baseball field with Ryan Braun, a superstar who was the National League Rookie of the Year in 2007 and voted its Most Valuable Player four years later in 2011. What could possibly be more enjoyable and exciting for Perrin than that.

Driving home from dinner that evening, I told Perrin that, given his intelligence, determination and curiosity, I thought he could have become a baseball player, an investment advisor, a lawyer or even a brain surgeon if he wanted to. Yet, having heard the joy in Perrin's voice and seeing the excitement on his face while describing his major league experience and his recent conversation with Ryan Braun, I was convinced that talking stocks on a baseball field with other ball players was truly his niche.

The next morning, after my yoga and meditation session, I grabbed some breakfast and made my way to Scottsdale Stadium for Cactus League's opening day where the Milwaukee Brewers were scheduled to play a split squad game against the San Francisco Giants. I passed through the turnstiles and immediately saw the starting lineups for each team displayed on the wall. I perused the batting orders and noticed several names that I was familiar with, each for a different reason.

Batting first for the Brewers was Eric Thames. I had recently read an article about Thames and how he learned to meditate during the years he played baseball overseas in South Korea. This was interesting to me because yoga and meditation have become an important part of my daily routine over the last several years. Batting third for the Brewers was Mauricio Dubon, whom I had admired from afar when he played short-stop for the Double-A minor league Biloxi Shuckers in 2017, on the same team with Perrin. I recalled Dubon's quickness on the base paths as he led the Shuckers in stolen bases before getting promoted to Triple-A Colorado Springs, the Brewers' top minor league team. Batting seventh for the Brewers was Lorenzo Cain, and batting eighth was Stephen Vogt, a catcher who I remembered well. Years ago, Vogt had tossed Nate two baseballs in a game when he was playing for the Oakland A's.

The starting pitcher for the Brewers that day was Aaron Wilkerson. Wilkerson had pitched with Perrin for the Biloxi Shuckers the prior year and was fortunate to get a late September call up to the Brewers' major league squad in 2017.

I became a big fan of Wilkerson when I learned that at one point in his life, he thought his baseball career was over due to injury. At that time, he worked in a grocery store stocking frozen food, while rehabbing his pitching arm back to health. With hard work and determination, he made a successful comeback. Wilkerson did more than come back to the game of baseball, he made it all the way to the show, the major leagues! Aaron Wilkerson, I salute you. May the Baseball Gods always be with you.

Pre-game, I saw Perrin emerge from the bullpen to warm-up with fellow Brewers pitcher Jorge Lopez. I found an empty seat in the first row and watched them toss the ball to one another. This warm-up is a ritual all ballplayers do before a practice or a game.

Seeing Perrin and Lopez tossing the ball to each other during their warmup brought back fond memories of playing catch with my dad in front of our home in Merrick, New York, when I was a kid. My dad would throw grounders and I would pretend to be Don Mattingly. Then he would throw pop-ups and I was Dave Winfield. Mattingly and Winfield, two true baseball greats, were my favorite New York Yankees back then. This tradition has been passed down to the next generation. Now I play catch with Nate in front of our home every chance we get. I also rooted for the New York Mets in those days, so I often pretended to be Mookie Wilson stealing a base or Lenny Dykstra diving to make a great catch in the outfield. One of my most memorable baseball moments as a Mets fan occurred when I went to Game 1 of the 1986 World Series with my uncle, Dr. Gary Koslow, the year the Mets won the championship.

Baseball fans will best remember the 1986 World Series for another reason. It was in Game 6 of that series that Bill Buckner let a ground ball pass under his glove and between his legs for an error that permitted the Mets to go on to defeat the Boston Red Sox to win the championship. It is unfortunate because Buckner was known as a real nice guy and was a great baseball player. He played in the majors for 22 seasons, won a batting title in 1980 with the Chicago Cubs, and was a National League all-star the next year. However, he will always be associated with that fielding error. Sometimes the Baseball Gods act in a way that mystifies us all.

When Perrin's warm-up with Lopez was over, he came over to say hello and tossed me the baseball they were using. I looked at the ball and noticed the Arizona 2018 MLB special logo embossed on it. My first thought was how excited Nate, a ballhawk, would be to receive this ball when I got home.

On the way toward my assigned seat for the start of the game, I saw Brewers outfielder and former Colorado Sky Sox minor leaguer, Brett Phillips, at the railing near the dugout graciously signing autographs. I lined up with the eager fans and when I got to Phillips, I told him that I would be giving the ball in my hand to my son and that a Brett Phillips signature on it would make it even more special. I thanked Phillips for the autograph and told him that I was grateful. As I walked away, signed ball in hand, I took the opportunity to thank the Baseball Gods for helping me acquire a perfect gift for Nate and a truly memorable souvenir from this trip to spring training in Arizona.

I would have loved it if Nate could have joined me on this adventure to see Perrin pitch in his major league debut in the

Cactus League, especially since Perrin had spent some time with my boy the past winter teaching him how to pitch. But with Nate's school and other activities, that was not possible. However, as I looked at the signed Cactus League ball in my hand, I thought about all the memorable baseball moments Nate and I have shared and I was grateful to have such a great gift to bring home to him.

As I approached the Brewers dugout to find my seat, I noticed Lorenzo Cain standing in front of it. I was close enough for him to hear me yell, "Lorenzo, we miss you in Kansas City!" Cain smiled, waved in recognition, and said, "Thanks." At that moment I realized once again just how special it was to see my favorite team, the Kansas City Royals, win the 2015 World Series.

Just before Perrin came into the game, I thought about the moment Nate and I shared in the upper deck of Kauffman Stadium, with two outs in the bottom of ninth inning of Game 7 of the 2014 World Series. The last out of that game was an infield pop-up that landed in the glove of the San Francisco Giants third baseman, who easily made the catch to end the Royals' amazing 2014 season and playoff run. As the Giants players swarmed the field to celebrate their hard-fought victory, Nate and I, along with the thirty-seven thousand Kansas City Royals fans, felt the emotional pain of losing a World Series Game 7 at home. I will never forget the name of the man who made that catch for the Giants to end the baseball season—Pablo Sandoval.

Perrin emerged from the bullpen in the second inning, as expected, and began his warm-up throws. As the first batter walked up to home plate, Perrin knelt down behind the pitcher's mound and with his finger drew his late sister Jennifer's initials into the dirt, an emotional pre-game ritual Perrin performs in her memory every time he pitches. Jennifer Perrin was killed by a drunk driver in a terrible car accident years ago. I have a feeling the Baseball Gods are watching, and smiling every time Perrin does this to honor his sister.

Perrin stood ready on the mound for his first pitch as the lead-off batter for the Giants was digging his cleats into the dirt in the batter's box. The batter was none other than Pablo Sandoval, the same player who had caught the pop up for the last out of the 2014 World Series years ago. Sandoval, a switch hitter, made Perrin work, but Perrin struck him out. Was that another wink from the universe, I wondered?

I was optimistic that Perrin's first outing in the Cactus League would be successful, especially after he struck out veteran Sandoval to start the inning. However, things quickly slipped out of control. Starting with the next batter, Perrin got hit hard, very hard, batter after batter. Then he threw a wild pitch. Then he gave up another hit. Perrin tried his best to keep his cool on the mound, but you could tell he was upset with his last few pitches and was certainly disappointed by the quick turn of events. So was I.

After the game, I saw a tweet from sports fan Andrew Wagner that vividly described Perrin's outing: "Things are not getting any better for Jon Perrin. A sac fly, single, wild pitch and then a 2-run double chase him with 2 outs in the 2nd. Giants 4, Brewers 2." Before the second inning was over, the Brewers' pitching coach came out of the dugout and signaled to the bullpen for another relief pitcher. The coach had seen enough that day, pulling Perrin from the mound before he even completing an inning.

Perrin dejectedly handed the ball to the pitching coach as he left the mound, walking slowly back to the dugout, head down in disappointment. Like Perrin, I was stunned by what had just happened. Perrin's pitching debut went from great to terrible so quickly. This was his first opportunity to pitch on the big stage and, like a bolt of lightning across the night sky, it was over in a flash. I pondered what could he or I had done to upset the Baseball Gods. Clearly, they had thrown Perrin a curve.

CHAPTER THREE

The Rookie

"Every day is the craziest."
—Shohei Ohtani

MY DAY AFTER PERRIN'S CACTUS LEAGUE DEBUT BEGAN very much like the day before. I did my yoga and meditation session by the pool in the morning just as the sun was rising to welcome another beautiful day in Arizona. After a quick shower and some breakfast, I stuffed my backpack with my baseball glove and the book that I was reading entitled *The Way of Baseball*, authored by ex-baseball player Shawn Green.

In his book, Green discusses how he discovered meditation and how it became his secret weapon in baseball and in life. I found the book so interesting and helpful that I believe it should be required reading for all young aspiring baseball players, and probably for everyone else trying to find their way on their life's path.

With Green's book in hand, I thought back to my own introduction to yoga and meditation. Years ago, I experienced a mid-life crisis. The stock market, particularly precious metals, precipitously decreased in value and many of my clients lost much of the gains that had previously accrued in their portfolios. This situation caused me to became depressed, angry and cynical. That's when I turned to yoga and meditation to get perspective and bring clarity and a new focus to my professional and personal life. It led me to a spiritual path that I have been on ever since. And to this day, I believe that yoga and meditation played a critical role in inspiring me to create Satya, my investment firm, to become an author, and helped me to discover that the Baseball Gods are real.

I had originally intended to catch a Royals game this day and cheer my favorite team to a spring training victory. But the Baseball Gods had other plans for me. Perrin texted me that the Brewers had another away game in Tempe, Arizona against the Los Angeles Angels and he took the liberty of reserving a ticket for me for that game. To my pleasant surprise, this game turned out to be particularly special for many baseball fans because the starting pitcher for the Angels was scheduled to be the young Japanese rookie sensation, Shohei Ohtani, known to many as the "Babe Ruth of Japan." Like the legendary Babe Ruth, who was a successful pitcher before becoming perhaps the greatest home run hitter of all time as an outfielder for the New York Yankees, Ohtani came to the major leagues here in America ready to succeed as a two-position player.

Babe Ruth pitched and played outfield for the Boston Red Sox when they won the World Series Championship in 1918. Ruth, who was just 23 at the time, started 19 games as a pitcher and 57 as an outfielder. That year he led the major leagues with

11 home runs and had an impressive 2.22 earned run average. He went on to win 3 World Series Championships with the Red Sox before being notoriously traded to their hated rivals, the New York Yankees. The Yankees went on to win 4 World Series with Ruth in their lineup.

Serious baseball fans are very familiar with Ruth's outstanding offensive statistics, like hitting 714 home runs and batting .342 for his career. But few know that the man, known as "The Bambino" and "The Sultan of Swat" because of his home run hitting prowess, was an outstanding pitcher as well. He had 94 wins and only 46 losses, a 67% winning percentage, and an ERA of 2.28 during his relatively short pitching career, quite an accomplishment.

The signing of international superstar Shohei Ohtani by the Los Angeles Angels brought with it much anticipation. American baseball is beloved in Japan and Japanese players, such as Hideki Matsui and Ichiro Suzuki, are considered living legends in their homeland. Japanese reporters and baseball fans desperately wanted Ohtani to succeed in the United States and all baseball lovers were curious to see if the Japanese superstar could make it in the major league in America, considered the best baseball league in the world.

Optimism for Ohtani's debut was high since he was coming off his best season in Japan. This 6-foot-3, left handed batting, right-handed pitching phenom was just a year removed from being voted the most valuable player of Japan's Pacific League at the young age of 22. According to Benjamin Hoffman's NY Times article, *Everything You Wanted to Know About Baseball's Intriguing Two-Way Player*, "In 2016, his last full season, he managed to be named to two different spots on the Pacific League's "Best 9" which honors the best player at each position. It is not hard to see why, considering Ohtani's impressive batting and pitching statistics that year."

I arrived at the Angels stadium in Tempe, parked the rental car, and looked around to find the entrance to the ballpark. I was somewhat disoriented because I was unfamiliar with the facility and the labyrinth parking lot didn't make my search any easier. At one point, I was stopped by security guards because, by mistake, I tried to enter the stadium at the gate entrance where the visiting team bus dropped off their players. The security guards probably thought I was trying to sneak into the ballpark! I must have had a look of confusion on my face when a woman walked up to me and asked if I was as lost as she was. We both laughed at our predicament and I suggested that we work as a team to find the proper entrance into the stadium.

I introduced myself and the woman replied that her name was Janet Horenstein. Like me, Janet was visiting Arizona to take in some spring training baseball games. Talking while walking, Janet noticed the Milwaukee Brewers jersey I had on and probably assumed I was a Brewers fan. I told her that I was a die-hard Royals fan, but also liked the Brewers.

While continuing our stroll to locate the entrance to the ballpark, I learned that Janet and her family were huge base-ball fans. She told me that her son worked for the Double-AA minor league team affiliated with the Detroit Tigers. Also, her family often hosted baseball players in the summer months if they needed a place to stay in southern California when they were in town for baseball training and related activities.

In response, I told Janet how I met Jon Perrin, how we had

become friends and colleagues, how I learned that he was a pitcher on the Biloxi Shuckers' Double-AA roster last year, and that Perrin was the reason I was at the game today. Janet then told me that a fellow Shucker, right fielder Clint Coulter, was one of the players that lived with her and her family for two months last summer. This "small world" story continued when I told Janet that I had actually met Clint Coulter and that at the end of the Shuckers' season last year, Coulter, Perrin and I played blackjack together at the casino in my hotel in Biloxi.

I questioned whether meeting Janet in the parking lot and conversing with her about baseball was a coincidence. More likely, it was another wink from the universe. When we finally reached the box office to pick up our tickets, we said goodbye and I entered the stadium to watch the debut of Shohei Ohtani, possibly the next Babe Ruth.

Despite the hype, Ohtani had an inauspicious debut and did not pitch very long. Interestingly, the most memorable performance of the day belonged to the starting pitcher for the Brewers, Brandon Woodruff, a rookie who also played with Perrin for the Biloxi Shuckers last season. Woodruff threw hard and his fastball left an impression on me, clocking in at 97, 98 and even 99 miles per hour on the radar gun. Woodruff pitched well and looked poised to make a huge upward move this season. I thought that he would likely be promoted to the Brewers' Triple-A Sky Sox squad this year and, if he performed as well there, might have a chance to make it to the majors. This was prophetic because Woodruff blossomed in Triple-A and, after getting called up to the Brewers major league team late in the season, he had a huge impact on the teams' playoff run against the Colorado Rockies and the Los Angeles Dodgers.

Sitting in my seat watching Ohtani and Woodruff duke it out on the diamond, I turned to the man next to me and started a conversation. I learned that he was a scout for the Oakland A's. We chatted about baseball, his job and the life of a scout. He had some funny and interesting stories to tell. Afterwards, however, I realized that the life of a scout was not easy or glamourous. It required endless travel, many long, boring days of driving, several weeks a year away from home, family and friends, and living out of a suitcase, often in hotels that may not have a 4-star rating from AAA. It's not unlike being a member of a touring rock band, just without the fame, fortune and the groupies.

This conversation with the scout reminded me of my experience as a music industry manager over two decades ago, one of the jobs I had after graduating from college. I worked for Alicia Gelernt's music management company at the time, with singer Patti Rothberg as one of its up and coming clients. Patti was asked to open for The Black Crows, one of my favorite rock bands since I was a teenager, during their upcoming 1997 European tour. Patti agreed to the gig and for two weeks I got to travel with Patti and the Black Crows on Patti's tour bus, watch their concerts from back stage in Spain, France, Germany and the Netherlands, and had the time of my life doing so.

Before the Brewers game ended, I asked the Oakland scout if he knew Jon Perrin and he said he did. Then I asked him if he thought Perrin would make it to the big leagues. He responded confidently, maybe a call up late this season, but next year for sure. Pleased with the knowledge that Perrin was on the radar screen of major league scouts, and delighted by the scout's analysis of his prospects, I left the stadium that day with a big smile on my face.

I met Perrin for dinner after the game near his apartment. Putting baseball aside for the moment, we began a work session to familiarize Perrin with Satya's back-office software. I was showing him how to use the different software tools that support Satya's investment management platform when something we heard on the television got our attention. Lifting our eyes from our laptops to focus on the ballgame on the screen, we saw that the Seattle Mariners had just brought in a new pitcher, Mike Morin, a local kid from Overland Park, KS. Perrin knew Morin growing up in Kansas City and in my first baseball book, I mentioned that Perrin and I had attended a Royals game together when Morin made his Kansas City Royals debut at Kauffman Stadium. We looked at each other, smiled, and acknowledged that this was probably the work of the Baseball Gods, winking from the universe. We ate our Greek food, got right back to work reviewing the features of Satya's client relationship management software, while Mike Morin pitched away in the background without all the hype that accompanied Shohei Ohtani's debut.

Even though Ohtani's Cactus League debut was uninspiring, he went on to have a terrific rookie season for the Los Angeles Angels. Despite struggling through injuries, Ohtani pitched really well. He had a 4-2 won-loss record, a 3.31 ERA and had 63 strike outs in 51.2 innings pitched. As a hitter, Ohtani did not disappoint, performing admirably for a rookie, posting a .285 batting average along with 22 home runs and 61

RBI's in only 326 at-bats. As a result of his impressive performance, both as a pitcher and as a hitter, Ohtani was named the
2018 American League Rookie of the Year!

CHAPTER FOUR

The Clubhouse

"He's a really smart kid. He's really doing stuff. Good for him."
—Brent Suter

IN LATE FEBRUARY 2018, TODD ROSIAK WROTE AN ARTICLE published in the *Milwaukee Journal Sentinel* entitled "Brewers prospect Jon Perrin is more than just a pitcher." The article discussed Perrin attending the Milwaukee Brewers spring training camp and mentioned that while focused on advancing up the ladder as a pitcher in the Brewers' organization, Perrin found time for non-baseball activities, such as tweeting about the stock market, politics, immigration, college sports, and even about the opioid crisis. The article also mentioned Perrin's desire to attend law school in the future, when his plate wasn't full of baseball and finance. The point clearly made was that Perrin was a pretty smart, well-rounded individual who happened to be a pretty good pitcher.

The Rosiak article featured one of Perrin's tweets from a few days earlier: "Just because you are an athlete does not make you ignorant. Just because you went to college does not mean you are educated. LeBron James is not only a successful athlete, but a successful business man as well. He is a self-made billionaire. #DontJustShutupAndPlay #AthleteAdvocacy." While the article focused primarily on his non-baseball interests and his law school aspirations, the Perrin tweets featured in Roziak's piece showcased his intellect and passion.

Perrin's intelligence and passion for the stock market was evident in the Brewers clubhouse as well. Perrin strived to be the first player to arrive in the clubhouse every day and the last to leave. This gave him time to review his investment portfolio and research new investment ideas before, in between, and after his baseball games and workouts. Whenever time permitted, Perrin would be in front of his laptop checking stock prices and reading articles about the latest economic and geopolitical developments. While some Brewers players and personnel simply took casual notice, others expressed interest in Perrin's financial endeavors and often asked him for investment advice. Well into the spring training season, Perrin had garnered enough interest among his teammates that some veteran players saw this as an opportunity to pull a clubhouse prank on the rookie, a somewhat controversial baseball ritual.

One day Perrin innocently walked into the Brewers locker room, as he had done pretty much every day for the previous six weeks. He was probably enjoying another beautiful, sunny Arizona morning as he hi-stepped into the clubhouse anticipating how neat and clean his locker would be when he got there. However, this morning would be different than all the others. To Perrin's surprise, just outside of the clubhouse bathroom, in front of a large garbage can, stood a recently constructed makeshift business office. Upon closer scrutiny,

Perrin saw a large, white sign hanging over the garbage can that read "J. Perrin Investment Group, open M-F 7-9pm." It was a fabricated investment office with a makeshift desk, a chair, an oversized calculator, a container of pencils and pens, a three-whole puncher, a large, old fashioned push-button phone, and the money section of USA Today. In Perrin's case, this long-held baseball tradition of hazing a rookie was well received and considered by all as an innocent prank, an inside joke, pulled off by friends.

When I learned about the Perrin hazing incident, I couldn't help but think back to my college days at Tulane as a freshman when I pledged a fraternity. I too was hazed, but not by baseball players. I was put through the ringer by my soon-to-be fraternity brothers. I look back now on those happy, memorable days pledging my fraternity, even the hazing, with love and affection. I suspect Perrin will remember his rookie locker room hazing the same way.

As the day progressed, I heard that sports writers on the Brewers beat were hunting down the Jon Perrin hazing story. Like FBI detectives involved in a criminal investigation, the sports writers probed players in the locker room to find out who was the mastermind behind the plot. Hints about which players instigated the prank started to surface. It was discovered that the culprits were pitcher Brent Suter, catcher Stephen Vogt, closer Corey Knebel, and relief pitcher Matt Albers. This was the group that conspired to poke a bit of fun at their blossoming in-house investment advisor and rookie teammate. It did not take long for the Brewers sports writers to turn the prank into a cover story. Perrin, with his good sense of humor, knowing that the prank was a sign of friendship and acceptance, took it all in stride.

At least three additional articles surfaced focusing on Perrin's new investment advisory career and the clubhouse prank that accompanied it. It was a surreal moment for me when I saw the article written by Alyson Footer featured on MLB.com at the top of the Brewers news section entitled, *"Brewers Get Last Laugh on Their "Gordon Gekko."* Making it onto MLB.com's website made the Perrin clubhouse prank an even bigger deal than I originally thought.

Footer's article fully captured the incident and included a couple of great quotes. Perrin observed, "This does kind of look like a Gordon Gekko situation," in reference to the classic film about Wall Street, a fictional tale about stock market manipulation and insider trading. Charlie Sheen starred as the young, up-and-coming stockbroker full of ambition, and Michael Douglas portrayed the iconic corporate raider Gordon Gecko, full of greed. Perrin displayed his humble nature and sense of humor when he told reporters, "I'm kind of a nerd. If you couldn't tell by the glasses." Needless to say, Perrin wears eyeglasses both on and off the baseball field.

What I liked best about the Footer article was its description of the prank as a sign of respect by Perrin's teammates. Pitcher Brent Suter, for example, was quoted in the article saying, "He's a really smart kid. He's really doing stuff. Good for him. It was kind of a fun joke, but I'm not exactly kidding when I ask him about stocks. I do ask him how they're doing."

During Suter's interview with reporters, he revealed that he may have been the ring leader of the clubhouse prank. Suter said, "He brings his laptop to meals, so a couple guys got together and decided we needed to give him his own space over there, his own little office. It looks like he's really taken to it." In the video of the interview, you can see Suter with a smile on his face. Clearly, he was pleased to see that the clubhouse prank on his good friend received wide media attention.

No doubt Suter, the probable mastermind behind the prank, has a good sense of humor as does Perrin. It turns out, these two gentlemen share some other interesting similarities as well.

Like Perrin, who played baseball and football, Suter thrived at two sports in high school. During his four years playing high school basketball, Suter's team won four consecutive conference titles, a state championship, and an amazing 85 out of 90 games. Suter's baseball team won three conference titles and made it to their state final four, with Suter named to the All-League and All-City teams. Also, like Perrin, Suter was not heavily recruited to play baseball coming out of high school. However, after he sent the baseball staff a video of him dunking a basketball, Suter got the attention of one of the most prestigious academic institutions in the world, Harvard University. Like all good manifestors, Suter did not just envision the college he wanted to go to, he took action to make his dream of attending that university come true.

Harvard was a great fit for Suter because he wanted to play college-level baseball and also obtain a high-quality education that would stay with him long after his baseball career was over. I was intrigued to learn that Suter studied environmental science and public policy while at Harvard, two subjects that both Perrin and I find important and interesting. While Perrin may be the only licensed registered investment advisor currently in baseball, Suter has the distinction of being the only active major league ball player to have graduated from Harvard.

Searching the internet, I stumbled upon a podcast interview of Suter entitled *The MindStrong Project*. Suter was featured in Episode 7 of the podcast, "Man of Many Talents." In the interview I learned that Suter was a religious man who found time for prayer and meditation every day. With regard to meditation, Suter said he meditated for thirty minutes a day, twice on game days. Suter said that meditation and prayer are the two cornerstones of his daily routine. He also said that he tried to find time to read the Bible every day. In addition, Suter told the podcast hosts that he always maintains a positive attitude, takes a high energy approach to his daily life, has a personal mantra of "No complaining during the day," and believes in living in a constant state of gratitude. Finally, Suter said that he makes sure to get a good night's sleep and eat healthy.

I was impressed to learn that Suter, like Perrin visualizes how he prepares, practices and pitches before every game. Suter believes that mental, physical, and spiritual preparation helps to turn what was visualized into reality. Their similarities don't end there. Suter, again like Perrin, is blessed with some unique pitching attributes that have helped him find success at the major league level. In my search, I found an interesting article written by Ryan Romano entitled "Three Unique Things About Brent Suter." Romano points out that in 2017, Suter had the slowest four-seam fastball velocity in the major leagues. Suter's average fastball clocked in at just 86.5 miles per hour, compared to the league average of 92.8 mph. To make matters more compelling, Suter's fastball spin rate is the sixteenth lowest in the big leagues, his vertical movement is fourth lowest, and his horizontal movement is eight lowest. Yet, somehow, Suter's fastball is remarkably effective.

Some analysts credit Suter's uncanny pitching success to several factors, such as his fast pace on the mound between pitches, his left-handed pickoff throw, and his unusual pitching windup. Suter's tricky windup is so unique that it even earned him the nickname "The Raptor," because his pitching motion resembles that of a raptor dinosaur. Suter's raptor pitching motion helps disguise his pitches and keeps even some of the best hitters in baseball off balance.

Suter, a low draft pick like Perrin, defied the odds as he climbed the ranks of the minor leagues on his road to the show. Suter, again like Perrin, has a prudent back-up plan just in case things don't work out on the baseball field, He has a college degree from Harvard, and Perrin is a registered investment advisor. Suter and Perrin both know that a career in baseball can be taken away by age, competition, injury or inefficiency, but a college degree or investment license stays with you long after your baseball playing days are over.

Brent Suter has blazed a trail for his buddy, Jon Perrin, to follow, and both have set a great example for all young student athletes in high school. While it may be tempting for a young, talented athlete to want to sign a contract with a big-league club right out of high school, it might be more prudent to go to college and earn a degree first. I suspect that Suter and Perrin would agree with me. Brent Suter, may the Baseball Gods always be with you.

On March 9, 2018, like poor Cinderella at the stroke of midnight in the famous fairy tale, Perrin was sent down to minor league spring training camp for the remainder of the Cactus League season. Gone were the days of spotless locker rooms, fine dining, and conversations with major league players about baseball, finance and investing. While Perrin remained in Arizona, I flew home. But I was not at home for long. Shortly thereafter, I was on my way with my family to visit spring training in south Florida, known as the Grapefruit League.

CHAPTER FIVE

The Grapefruit League

"Setting goals is the first step in turning the invisible into the visible."
—Tony Robbins

ABOUT HALF OF THE MAJOR LEAGUE BASEBALL TEAMS play their Spring training games in the Arizona Cactus League. The other half play in Florida in the Grapefruit League. While I had never really given it much thought before, it makes sense for the teams from the northeast, such as the New York Yankees, New York Mets, and Boston Red Sox, to locate spring training down south in Florida, while teams from the central part of the country, such as the Kansas City Royals, Milwaukee Brewers, and Detroit Tigers, and the west coast, such as the Los Angeles Angels and San Francisco Giants, have spring training in Arizona.

The Baseball Gods must have whispered this information to my parents because, in 2016, they purchased a retirement home in Delray Beach, Florida. Delray Beach is located about an hour north of Miami, and, more important to Nate and me, about thirty minutes south of The Ballpark of the Palm Beaches, the recently built, state-of-the-art stadium that hosts both the Washington Nationals and the Houston Astros for spring training.

My family and I were really looking forward to our visit to my parents during the kids' spring break vacation from school. Reggie was looking forward to some rest and relaxation on the beach in the warm Florida sun. My daughter, Kayla, was looking forward to working out at the gym, playing bocce and pickleball with her Grandpa, and hanging out at the pool. Nate was daydreaming about ballhawking at his first spring training game in Florida and I was thinking about how grateful I was to be able to go to a ballgame with both my dad and my son. On top of all this, we were getting to spend some quality vacation time with my parents.

After two days of fun in the sun, it was time for the boys to see some baseball. The first game my dad, Nate and I attended had the New York Mets playing against the Washington Nationals. As the three of us walked up to pick up our tickets at the box office, I noticed a Mets fan in front of us. What caught my attention was her bright orange Mets T-shirt. A closer look revealed the number 30 with the name "Scooter" above the number. I fast-stepped up to the woman, tapped her on the shoulder, and asked who wears the number 30 on the Mets. She replied, "Michael Conforto and his nickname is Scooter." At the time, I didn't know that there was more than one ball player with the nickname "Scooter," the nickname my dad gave to me when I was a kid. I only knew of Scooter Gennett, formerly with the Milwaukee Brewers and the Cincinnati Reds, but recently traded to the San Francisco

Giants. It was a nice wink from the universe. The Baseball Gods were clearly with me that day at the ballpark.

We picked up our tickets at the box office and entered this new spring training baseball cathedral. In appreciation, I made a namaste, a yoga peace gesture, to the ticket taker as I walked through the turnstile. Before we could say hello to the three giant-headed mascots of former U.S. presidents who greet fans as they enter the ballpark, and later tour the stadium during the game, Nate was off to the all-grass outfield stands where his ballhawk daydreams once again came to life.

Nate hawked his first ball of his Grapefruit League spring training season within the first five minutes of batting practice! He caught his second ball a few minutes later and, immediately thereafter, another. Nate was in ballhawk baseball heaven.

After Nate snagged three baseballs in ten minutes, we were very surprised to see some familiar faces at the ballpark. Walking in our direction were Dr. Steven Rosenberg and his son, Jordan, Nate's friend from Kansas City and a fellow ballhawk. The Rosenberg's were in town visiting grandma and they had just come from batting practice on another field where Jordan had no competition hawking for balls. As Jordan approached us, we couldn't help but notice that he was struggling to use his shirt as a bucket to hold about a dozen baseballs. Jordan had just hit the ballhawk jackpot.

I first met Steve Rosenberg at the home of our friends, Justin and Meg Shaw, when we were invited to their annual Super Bowl party shortly after we moved from New York to Kansas City. Nate and Jordan's friendship blossomed during the summer of 2013 at camp. The four of us even hit golf balls at a driving range one time and later attended a Royals game together at Kauffman Stadium. It was at that Royals game that Nate and I introduced Jordan and Steve to the art of ball-hawking. Both Nate and Jordan caught toss-up balls that day and Jordan has been an avid ballhawk ever since.

While our sons were ballhawking, and later during the Royals game, Steve and I discussed a wide range of topics. We talked baseball, the stock market, and how much we both liked living in Kansas City even though we were raised on the east coast. I also discussed with Steve my passion for yoga and my renewed interest in daily meditation. That's when Steve told me that he used to practice Transcendental Meditation, the mysterious method known as "TM."

I experimented with different meditation techniques for several years and was very curious to learn more about TM. While unfamiliar with the specific technique, I did know that TM was developed by the Indian guru Maharishi Mahesh Yogi. Maharishi, as he was commonly known, brought his teachings to the west, and his popularity exploded after he befriended the Beatles in the 1960s. Steve explained to me how TM works, and I became even more intrigued because it seemed so simple.

Despite acknowledging the benefits of a daily TM practice, Steve told me that he had stopped meditating a few years ago. However, Steve said that without his daily TM, he noticed changes in himself, like becoming more easily stressed from the burdens of his large workload. To be fair, Steve has the responsibility of running a rehabilitation facility for the elderly in Kansas City, which carries with it not only operational stress but emotional stress as well. Interestingly, Steve told me then when he returned to a daily meditation practice, his entire reality began to shift and improve. Even though he had given up meditation for years, Steve quickly regained his Zen-like state of mind when he restarted, just like riding a bike. Speaking with Steve about meditation was a reminder of how important it was for me to keep up with my own daily practices, even while on vacations.

Although we hadn't seen each other for some time, there we were, together again, just shooting the breeze and talking about life at a baseball game as our boys' ballhawked in the distance. Our conversation seemed to pick up right where it had left off months ago. The only difference was that we were enjoying the backdrop of palm trees at The Ballpark of the Palm Beaches in Florida rather than the famous water fountains at Kauffman Stadium at home.

Nate and I said goodbye to the Rosenberg's and found our way to the third base line where Mets players were warming up before the game. A few players, done with stretching and playing catch, made their way over to the legion of Mets fans against the rail begging for autographs. Todd Frazier, the Mets third baseman, was nice enough to sign for the fans, including one of the baseballs Nate had recently ballhawked.

Then Ty Kelly, a multi-position player then with the Mets but now with the Los Angeles Angels organization, came by and started signing autographs for fans right in front of us. Kelly was signing another one of Nate's baseballs when I noticed a blue, rubber bracelet on his wrist. A closer look revealed an Israeli flag on it. Surprised, I said to Kelly, "Hey, are you Jewish?" Kelly responded that his mom is Jewish and that he actually played baseball for the Israel national team during the recent World Baseball Classic tournament. He told us that a number of American Jews played for Israel's national team since there were not yet enough talented Israeli baseball players to compete at the major league level.

That night after the Mets-Nationals game, I brought my yoga mat poolside at our hotel and did a session next to a hot tub that was surrounded by a waterfall. The moon was out and the stars were shining particularly brightly, giving the ocean a nice shimmering glow. After I did some yoga flows, I laid down on my back and stared at the stars. Occasionally airplanes would fly by and slowly glide through the gentle night sky. I took four deep breaths, closed my eyes, silently recited my daily mantra, and I was at peace with the world.

When I returned to our hotel room, something very exciting happened. I received a text message from Jon Perrin telling me that he had just signed his first client to Satya Investment Management! As fate would have it, Perrin's first client was a professional baseball player.

Perrin's text reminded me of a day years ago when I had the opportunity to play a round of golf with my father-in law, Sam, and retired baseball players Joe Carter and Joe Randa. Perhaps I was delirious or simply exhausted from 103-degree heat that day, but driving home I had a vision that one day I would leave Morgan Stanley, start my own investment firm, and manage money for baseball players. Thanks to Jon Perrin, my Satya prophecy had become a reality.

Before the family returned home to Kansas City, my dad, Nate and I attended one more Grapefruit League game. This time we saw the Washington Nationals play against the defending World Series champion Houston Astros. Nate was really looking forward this outing, given the success he had ballhawking at the last game. Unfortunately, this game was well attended and Nate struggled to hawk a ball. He was shut out during batting practice and, even though he remained optimistic that he would catch a home run ball during the game, the Baseball Gods were not kind to Nate this day. He left the stadium empty handed and was frustrated with his lack of ballhawking success. I wanted to tell Nate that he was starting to take his ballhawk career a little too seriously, but before I could, he told me that this was the first game since becoming a ballhawk that he didn't get a ball and that his consecutive game streak was now over. I decided to leave this between Nate and the Baseball Gods. I put my arm around his shoulder and said, "Hey cheer up. I have a feeling that we will be coming back to the Grapefruit League real soon."

CHAPTER SIX

The Fantasy Baseball League

"When you teach your son, you teach your son's son"
—The Talmud

IN HIGH SCHOOL I JOINED A FANTASY BASKETBALL LEAGUE
and, years later in college, I participated in a fantasy football
league. In 2018, thanks to the writers at the website Reviewing
the Brew, I got the opportunity to "own" a team in a fantasy
baseball league. Being a huge fan and an avid follower of baseball, this was very good news for me.

This opportunity actually arose weeks earlier when I visited
Perrin in Arizona during his major league spring training stint
with the Brewers. On my computer going through emails in
my hotel room in Phoenix, I noticed an email with the following subject line: "You're invited to join an ESPN Fantasy
Baseball League."

A few weeks prior to that, I had responded, on Twitter, to
a request to enter a fantasy baseball league run by the website.
The staff writers had created a new league and wanted half of
the "team owners" to be Brewers fans. While officially a true

Royals loyalist, I had become a semi-Brewers fan due to my friendship with Perrin. I also felt sufficiently qualified because I liked and followed the Brewers and their minor league affiliates, the Colorado Springs Sky Sox, the Biloxi Shuckers, and the Carolina Mudcats, on a regular basis. I made my case in an email response to the league commissioner in which I also mentioned that I was an author in the process of writing a book series about baseball.

When I received the acceptance notification from the fantasy league commissioner, I felt like I had just been given a bid to join a college fraternity. I remember Face Timing with Nate from my hotel room to tell him the good news and asked him if he wanted to become a "co-owner" and manage a fantasy baseball team with me. He immediately agreed and we decided to name our team "The Satya Baseball Gods."

For our "rookie" baseball fantasy league season, Nate wanted me to run the day-to-day operations of our team and he would be in charge of our fantasy draft. I agreed. On draft night, I set up our dining room as if it were a professional draft day war room. I laid out research reports and player rankings at each position. I sat behind my laptop computer like a sabermetrics guru while Nate got his chance to experience draft day, one of the most important tasks of being a baseball general manager, just like Dayton Moore of the Kansas City Royals and David Stearns of the Milwaukee Brewers. Nate sat like a baseball oracle, waiting to be asked questions about which player should be our next selection and why. As the time for each of our draft picks approached, I would tell Nate which players were still available. Then, when it was our turn to select, I would give him two or three names to choose from.

Whichever player Nate selected, we drafted. Nate and I had a lot of fun working together and building our team roster as the night went on, and I thought we did a pretty good job.

Our first pick was Clayton Kershaw, pitching ace for the Los Angeles Dodger and three-time Cy Young Award winner in the National League. Our second pick was Yankee power hitter Aaron Judge. Late in the draft, we selected Ian Kennedy, who pitches for the Royals and happens to be our neighbor down the block. We also selected some of our other favorite Royals, including Salvador Perez, Whit Merrifield, Jorge Soler, and new Royals first baseman Lucas Duda. To complete our team, we selected Robinson Cano, who years ago tossed Nate a pre-signed baseball, and with our last pick, we took Taylor Williams, Jon Perrin's good friend and former roommate, now a relief pitcher for the Brewers.

On opening day of the regular baseball season, Nate and I were at Kauffman Stadium to see the game and, as usual, Nate caught a toss-up ball. We were particularly excited to be at the K that day because we were going to see many of the Kansas City Royals players we had selected for our fantasy baseball team. When Lucas Duda came to the plate, his first at bat of the season and also his first career at-bat with the Royals, we cheered for him to hit a home run, and he did! Our celebration was two-fold, first for our team, the Kansas City Royals, and then for our fantasy baseball league team, the Satya Baseball Gods.

CHAPTER SEVEN

The Minor League You've Never Heard Of

"One Step Forward, Two Steps Back."
—Bruce Springsteen

WITH THE END OF SPRING TRAINING, THE 2018 MAJOR league baseball season was now underway. The Brewers organization had selected their 25-man roster to complete their opening day major league squad. The remaining Brewer players, those who didn't make it to the show, were assigned to affiliate minor league teams in Triple-A, Double-A and Single-A.

I was disappointed, and frankly somewhat surprised, to learn that Jon Perrin was left off of the Brewers Colorado Springs Sky Sox Triple-A roster in the Pacific Coast League. Curiously, Perrin was not on the Brewers Biloxi's Double-A roster either. Apparently, Perrin was left off all of their minor league affiliate rosters and I wondered if something was wrong. Unfortunately, instead of beginning the season in Triple-A, Perrin began the year in the minor league you've never heard of, known as "extended spring training." Just as his investment management career was taking off on the runway, Perrin's baseball career had stalled at the gate.

At the end of spring training, Perrin told me that he did not break camp with the rest of the team and, instead, had been assigned to extended spring training. I had never heard that term before, despite following baseball for decades. I learned that extended spring training is, in most respects, very much like regular spring training. Every day, players practice their daily routines, including batting and bunting, infield and outfield drills, spending time in the weight room, playing in intra-squad and inter-squad games, and, as in Perrin's case, working on mechanics. However, when extended spring training begins, gone are the fans, there are no kids at the railing seeking autographs, and there are no lines at the concession stands. When teams play each other, they don't even keep score. The only folks in the stands are scouts.

Extended spring training typically hosts a crew of baseball players with special circumstances. For some, it's like an oasis and for others, it's like a prison. For example, some players are on the disabled list and remain behind to rehabilitate an injury. Some younger players stay to gain experience or need additional time to mature before taking on the pressure and rigors of a full season in the majors. Others may be on temporary suspension by the league for taking illegal recreational or performance enhancing drugs and stay to remain in shape during their suspension. And there are some players who are being held back to work on their mechanics, such as a pitcher adding a new pitch to his repertoire, or a starting pitcher learning to become a middle reliever or a closer. Lastly, there may be some who are being disciplined for behavior deemed inappropriate or detrimental to the team by their organizations. So, while spending time in extended spring training was not necessarily a bad thing, I had a bad feeling.

The Brewers farm team director told Perrin that he needed to improve his pitching mechanics before heading out to Colorado Springs. While it sounded promising that Perrin would soon be on his way to the Sky Sox Triple-A squad, being told that he needed to "work on his mechanics" after just spending two months in spring training was a red flag and, in my view, not good news at all.

I contacted Perrin to get more information and find out what was going on. Initially, Perrin told me that he would remain in Arizona for just one week. However, after two weeks, I became concerned that there was more to this situation than I originally thought. After three weeks, I became convinced that Perrin was not being treating fairly because I thought he had earned the opportunity to be pitching in real minor league games. I even thought he might be getting disciplined for something that happened that I was not aware of. But what did I know about running a major league baseball franchise. My managerial experience was limited to co-ownership of a fantasy baseball team.

Perrin's situation was creating negative energy for me, and I knew that was not a good thing. Then, trying to be as optimistic as possible, my thoughts moved in a different direction. I wondered if Perrin was being held back in Arizona to keep him healthy. Perhaps the Brewers were keeping him back because they were thinking about trading him to another team, maybe to my beloved Royals. These positive thoughts were consistent with my view of the law of attraction and the power of positive thinking, which I now embrace. I had to erase negativity and prevent myself from slipping back into old, detrimental habits.

To make Perrin's situation even more difficult for me to accept, this was all happening to him at a time when some good things were happening to several of Perrin's baseball buddies. First, pitcher Adrian Houser, with whom Perrin had become friendly while they played together in the 2017 Arizona Fall League, was called up to the Brewers directly from Double-A Biloxi. In his first outing in the show, Houser pitched two innings and gave up no runs. Then Perrin's former roommate and good friend Taylor Williams got called up to the Brewers from Triple-A Colorado Springs. Shortly thereafter, Jorge Lopez, another friend and fellow pitcher, got called up to the big leagues with the Brewers.

Jorge Lopez had gotten my attention weeks prior after I read an article about him written by Tom Haudricourt in the *Milwaukee Journal Sentinel*. The article, entitled "A Survivor of Both Hurricane Maria and Career Challenges, Jorge Lopez Faces a Big Season," told an emotional tale that touched me deeply. Lopez was at his in-laws' home in Puerto Rico on September 20, 2017 when Hurricane Maria hit. As you may recall, Maria was a deadly category 5 hurricane that devastated Puerto Rico and other Caribbean islands in its path, and is regarded as one of the worst natural disasters on record affecting those islands. The rain came pouring down for days and the wind was fierce. Streets began to flood, trees were uprooted, roads became blocked, and many homes were destroyed. Then the power went out. Hurricane Maria pretty much destroyed everything in her wake. Puerto Rico would need many months to rebuild, and to this day the island has not yet fully recovered.

At that time, Lopez and his wife Karla's four-year-old son, Mikael, suffered from a hereditary inflammatory disorder that affects the lining of the abdomen, chest and joints called familiar Mediterranean fever. As a result, Mikael has needed special medical attention since birth. Fearing for his son's health and survival, Lopez made the tough decision to leave the rest of his family in Puerto Rico at this difficult, stressful time and moved to Miami to access medical treatment for Mikael. Lopez felt he had no choice. He had to do this to save his son.

Interested to learn more about Lopez, I read Adam McCalvy's MLB.com article entitled "Lopez's Turnaround has Brewers' Attention." The article noted that Lopez was a former second round draft pick and made it to the show as a 22-year-old at the end of the 2015 season. However, in 2016, he was sent back down to Triple-A where he struggled to adjust to the high altitude, cool temperatures, windy conditions and dry air of Colorado Springs. These weather conditions, coupled with the well-known hitter-friendly altitude and field dimensions of the ballpark, have caused many pitchers to struggle in Colorado Springs. These factors may have played a role in the decision for the Sky Sox to relocate to San Antonio, TX starting in 2019.

After he struggled in Triple-A in Colorado Springs, Lopez was sent back down to the Double-A Biloxi Shuckers, where he and Jon Perrin met and became friends. In the warm, humid air of Mississippi, Lopez responded well from his earlier career setback and regained his form as the season progressed. The 2016 season was a transition year for Lopez, but he finished strong, especially in the final five games he pitched for the Shuckers.

In the offseason, Lopez worked hard and found his groove again, in earnest, playing back home in Puerto Rico in the winter league where his pitching statistics were stellar. He returned to the Biloxi Shuckers in the spring back in form and well prepared for an outstanding comeback season. Lopez pitched well in 2017 and earned himself a brief call-up from the Brewers. For his first time since 2015, Lopez was back in the show. Jorge Lopez, may the Baseball Gods always be with you!

CHAPTER EIGHT

The Pacific Coast League

"Mr. Perrin here is a pitcher, and a stock market student,
analyst, investor. He is a capitalist."
—Keith Olbermann

AFTER LATE NIGHT DRAMA TO AVERT A GOVERNMENT
shutdown with less than 24 hours to spare, the Senate passed
a huge $1.3 trillion-dollar spending bill designed to fund the
government through September. Later the same day, President
Trump signed the bill into law.

Most politicians in the House of Representatives and
Senate were kept in the dark about many of the details of this
massive spending bill. Nevertheless, within hours of its writing, members of Congress were expected to vote "yes" to a
mammoth spending bill they did not even have time to read
and digest. With fear of a government shutdown looming, and
its political consequences, many Congressmen felt that they
had no choice but to approve the bill to keep the government
open for business.

The spending bill addressed many aspects of American life,

including authorizing substantial budget increases in defense and domestic spending. Hidden deep within the 2,232 pages of this spending package was an Orwellian provision, the "Save America's Pastime Act."

Simply, the Save America's Pastime Act allows major league baseball to continue to pay minor league players below minimum wage. Apparently, baseball team owners have lobbied Congress for years to get this bill passed into law. The baseball powers that be finally got their way when lawmakers quietly slipped this Act into the spending package, with only a few people interested in the provision paying attention. It reminded me of the time Congress passed the Federal Reserve Act more than a century ago, on December 23, 1913, just before Christmas Eve, when most politicians and political onlookers were busy with their families and getting their last-minute holiday shopping done.

The lobbyist hired by major league baseball owners argued that minor league baseball players are seasonal workers, not full-time employees like players in the majors. Therefore, the argument continued, they should be subject to a different set of rules and compensation. As seasonal workers, for example, they would not be entitled to overtime pay. This was a bogus argument since minor league players often play six or seven days a week and have extensive work and travel obligations during the season. Plus, most also train during the offseason or play winter ball to stay in shape. That sound full-time to me.

The lobbyists also argued that if baseball teams had to pay minor league players like full-time employees, their minor league affiliates would be asked to share the cost, which would force many of them out of business. However, since the major league clubs pay the salaries of the players, not the minor league affiliates, the argument is spurious. In his CBS Sports article "Congress' Save America's Pastime Act," Mike Axisa points out that "There are about 4,500 players on minor-league rosters. Paying each of them an extra $300 per month would equal another $8.1 million total for the season." Clearly, if major league clubs can afford to pay top players as much as $25 million per year for several seasons, they could easily find room in their budgets to pay minor league players much more, if they wanted to.

The passing of the Save America's Pastime Act seemed unfair to me, and given the name of the bill, ironically un-American as well. Yet, despite how inequitable this mandate seemed to be, most players would not dare speak up on such matters. Jon Perrin, however, is not your typical baseball player. I've learned that Perrin speaks his mind, and often uses social media, especially Twitter, to do so.

In response to the passage of this new law, Perrin tweeted, "The 'Save America's Pastime Act' is the US government providing a $10 billion industry an exemption from paying their employees a livable wage. My question is: what exactly are you saving?" Perrin also tweeted, "MLB Revenue grew for the 15th consecutive season in 2017 coming in at over $10 billion..." Perrin then posted a chart of major league baseball revenue over the last twenty years clearly showing that MLB has been a money-making machine over these years. In addition, the value of almost every major league baseball franchise has increased immeasurably over that period, further lining the pockets of their owners.

Perrin had more to say on the matter tweeting, "And here

are some fun facts about minor league baseball... Salaries have not even grown to cover the cost of inflation in the last 40 years." Now, on a roll like a freshly packed snowball going down a hill, Perrin could not be stopped tweeting another gem, "Minor League Baseball is living proof that trickle-down economics is a myth. More money at the top just stays at the top." Yikes, now Perrin was dissing not only major league baseball and its team owners, but also former President Ronald Reagan, a huge proponent of the macro-economic strategy known as supply-side economics, often called "Reaganomics."

Perrin's tweets caught the attention of former ESPN SportsCenter anchor and MSNBC political talk show host Keith Olbermann. To his more than one million Twitter followers, Olbermann retweeted Perrin's first tweet on this subject matter and added, "Mr. Perrin here is a pitcher, and a stock market student, analyst, investor. He is a capitalist." With one tweet, Perrin's outspoken views on this subject were getting some serious attention.

A few years ago, my college buddy and baseball aficionado Bobby Aguilera suggested I start listening to *Effectively Wild*, a FanGraphs baseball podcast. Taking Bobby's advice, I tuned into the podcast a few times and found it to be interesting and informative. I began listening to Ben Lindbergh and Jeff Sullivan on a regular basis to prepare for the upcoming fantasy baseball season. I thought Lindberg and Sullivan, who had great chemistry, were extremely knowledgeable and their baseball insights were thought-provoking. Plus, they also booked interesting and insightful guests to interview on their show.

This show took on greater relevance for me when I received

a text from Bobby with a link to its most recent podcast called "*Effectively Wild* Episode 1196: A Minor-League Pitcher Explains Minor-League Pay." When I clicked on the link, I was astonished to see that the interview of the day was with none other than Brewers minor league pitching prospect and Satya Investment Advisor Jon Perrin! Interestingly, the hosts began the interview by mentioning that other players had declined the opportunity to be interviewed to discuss the Save America's Pastime Act for fear of repercussions. When I heard that I thought, "Uh oh!" However, unlike most other players, Perrin has no fear and speaks, and tweets, his mind when it comes to important issues that matter to him.

In my opinion, Perrin seemed humble, intelligent, articulate and passionate during the podcast interview. He provided gritty details about the Save America's Pastime Act and discussed how little minor leaguers get paid, their poor locker room, travel and living conditions, and the struggle players face, especially those with families to support. Perrin gave suggestions for changes team owners could make that would improve conditions for minor leaguers, such as paying them a year-round salary rather than as seasonal employees during the months of the year baseball is played. Perrin made the case that while major league baseball and its owners who lobbied this bill into law made a savvy business move, it revealed a greedy nature and the unfair playing field that exists between owners and minor league players.

When asked about his potential future law career, Perrin said his focus was 100% on baseball right now, but he would like to pursue a law degree after his baseball days are over. When asked if he would consider becoming a lawyer and represent minor league players, Perrin responded with a definitive yes.

For the next several days I pondered the ramifications of Perrin's interview. On the one hand, I was impressed how well he conducted himself, and proud of his courage for speaking his mind on such matters. On the other hand, I feared Perrin may have put a mark on his back and could have jeopardized his baseball career by being so outspoken on such sensitive issues. I was worried that his interview may have upset team owners and, over the next several days, became increasingly concerned that Perrin might be "blackballed."

Blackballing is defined as the practice by a private organization of denying an individual or individuals seeking membership. The practice can be used to prevent a college student pledging a fraternity, and years ago, it was used in Hollywood to deny employment to actors, directors, screenwriters and other entertainment professionals because they were accused of being Communists. Historically, members in these organizations voted by secret ballots with a white ball signifying a yes vote or a black ball signifying a no vote. In some organizations, a single back ball would be enough to prevent a candidate from admission to the group.

In the modern sports world, there may be no better example of an athlete getting "blackballed" for a political view than National Football League quarterback Colin Kaepernick.

A few years ago, during the playing of the pre-game national anthem at an NFL game, rather than standing tall, saluting the American flag and singing along, a tradition held dear by patriotic Americans and avid football fans, Kaepernick chose to make a political statement by kneeling down to protest a rash of recent shootings and perceived police brutality in black communities across the country. I don't think his actions were intended to be a protest against America or its flag, but the NFL team owners, and later even President Trump, felt that Kaepernick's protest was unpatriotic and disrespectful to U.S. soldiers and veterans who have fought and died for our country. Kaepernick, who had very strong feelings on the issue, ignored his critics and continued to kneel during the national anthem at each game for the rest of the season.

To complicate matters, other NFL players began to follow Kaepernick's lead. Before the NFL knew it, players on almost every team were kneeling during the national anthem. When Kaepernick's contract with the San Francisco 49ers expired, he was not re-signed. More curiously, as a free agent, he could not land another job in the NFL despite being in the prime of his career. As months went by, reporters and fans began to suspect that Kaepernick had been "blackballed."

This conspiracy theory was supported in Jack Moore's article in the *Guardian*, "A Form of Punishment: Colin Kaepernick and the History of Blackballing in Sports." Moore describes a 2017 NFL free-agent market with Kaepernick still without an offer while many less talented players received lucrative deals, including unproven Mike Glennon, career backup Josh McCown, journeyman Brian Hoyer, Landry Jones and Matt Barkley. Also, a general manager anonymously told Mike Freeman of the *Bleacher Report* that roughly 70% of NFL teams were unwilling to sign Kaepernick, not because they didn't believe he could play, but as punishment for expressing his political beliefs. One team, the Seattle Seahawks, was willing to sign Kaepernick to a contract but insisted that he agree to stand for the national anthem during every game. When he refused, the Seahawks decided not to sign him and withdrew the offer.

This was not the first time a professional athlete has been blackballed for speaking out about controversial political beliefs. When Craig Hodges, a two-time National Basketball Association champion with the Chicago Bulls, voiced his opinion on a number of issues, including poverty in the black community in Chicago and his opposition to the first Gulf War, he found himself out of a job despite his brilliant 42.5% three-point shooting percentage over his four seasons with the Bulls. Hodges became a free agent but never played in the NBA again.

With this background, one day I asked Perrin if thought that he was being punished, or blackballed, for speaking his mind. He said no, he didn't think so. He believed management just wanted to keep him in Arizona for extended spring training to work on his mechanics. Then I reminded Perrin of what happened to Tyler Cravy and Rob Scahill the year before.

After I met Perrin and found out that he played baseball in the Brewers organization, I started to follow the team closely. I recall the odd turn of events when both Cravy and Scahill were unexpectedly cut by the Brewers at the end of spring training. Both veterans were told by team management that if they performed well in the Cactus League, they would be offered spots on the 25-man opening day roster. However, when the team broke camp, both were sent down to Triple-A despite having pitched exceptionally well. Cravy had an outstanding 2.03 ERA during the Cactus League games and, over his 11 outings, held opposing hitters to a ridiculously low .116 batting average. Scahill was equally terrific. He posted a 0.73 ERA, allowing only one run in 12 outings. Both players were more than disappointed when told that they did not make it to the show.

Cravy was particularly upset and chose to express his opinion. In an article by Tom Haudricourt with the headline "Pitcher Tyler Cravy Lashes Out After Being Cut by Brewers," Cravy is quoted saying a few things that he might have later regretted. For example, he said that rather than reporting to the minors, he might seek a 9 to 5 job where he would be treated like a human. Cravy may have been a little harsh with that comment, but he did make a solid argument. Cravy continued, "It would just be nice to have the honest straight up front instead of, 'Hey, you're competing for a job,' then literally out-compete everyone and be told, 'Sorry, we have other plans.'" Cravy could have stopped there but, instead, he kept the snowball rolling down the hill quipping, "It says a lot about the integrity, or lack thereof, of the guys running the show, but what are you going to do? All you can do is put up numbers and sometimes that's still not enough. I don't think they would release me. I think it would just be me deciding to quit if I chose that route. I'm just not sure I want to play for guys who treat you like this." I cannot say for sure whether Cravy got blackballed as a result of his comments, but despite pitching well in the majors in 2016 and in spring training, he has not played in another major league game.

The Haudricourt article points out that, unlike Cravy, Scahill took his demotion in stride. He is quoted saying "I'm not the one who makes the decisions. I'm not happy but it's part of the game. I understand that but it doesn't make it any easier." Scahill, not surprisingly, made it back to the show with the Chicago White Sox.

Shortly thereafter, I saw on Twitter that Perrin was asked to give another interview on the subject of "minor league pay." I texted Perrin suggesting that he decline the interview. Perrin responded that he had already accepted the interview and that he had no intention of discontinuing his efforts to speak out on important issues like minor league compensation and living conditions.

Perrin helped me see the light his way by sending a *Bloomberg* article, "This Disillusioned Banker Quit Barclays to Invest His Own Way," written by Shoko Oda and Yuko Takeo. The article featured Yasuyuki Kamata, a man who at the age of 43 became so disillusioned with Wall Street that he considered leaving the business. Rather than doing so, Kamata started his own money management firm that would do things differently. His firm would focus on sustainable, environmental, social and governance related investing. Kamata rejected traditional industry practices and let morality and integrity guide his career path. By letting his values and principles lead the way, he found peace of mind and rediscovered his love for investing.

Perrin, who understands me well, knew that I, like Kamata, also considered leaving the investment business because I too had become disillusioned. Like Kamata, I started Satya, my own socially responsible investment firm, and as part of its mission to do good by doing well, my firm contributes 10% of its profits to charitable organizations suggested by its clients. By forwarding the Kamata article to me, Perrin, speaking without words, convinced me that being outspoken, and doing the right thing, is part of his life's purpose. After the exchange of some additional texts, I stopped worrying about my "blackball conspiracy theory" and decided to get behind Perrin's mission 100%.

With these positive thoughts flowing, the day before my forty-fourth birthday *A Frugal Athlete* released the interview, "Money Talks with Jonathan Perrin." The segment focused on many things related to finance and baseball. After acknowledging that Perrin may be the only current professional athlete that is also a certified financial investment advisor, they asked him to talk about that process and what it was like taking the Series 65 exam. Perrin's reply gave me a feeling of pride and satisfaction.

"I'm not sure if I'm the only one certified or not, but I know for a fact that I'm certainly not the only person that is interested in investing and there are surprising number of players in the game that handle their own finances. The process for me taking the Series 65 exam to become a Registered Investment Advisor was the culmination of about three years of personal education in finance once I graduated college and signed my pro contract. I actually graduated from Oklahoma State University with a degree in history, and by the time I finished school and signed a professional contract I had very little education when it came to finance. I am an avid reader, so I began reading books on investing, finance, and general economics. After about a year and a half of research, combined with some saving that I had done over the first couple seasons of my career, I opened my own personal investment account. During that offseason I was actually working as a host in a restaurant when I met who is now my current boss: Jonathan Fink, of Satya Investment Management. He would come in for lunch a few times a week and would always be carrying some stacks of research reports with him. After a few days, I started chatting him up about what he was reading and started to give him my own input based on what I had learned from my own research. Eventually we met up for coffee and kept in touch over the course of the 2017 season. Then when I came back home for the offseason, he offered to hire me as an investment advisor and have his firm sponsor me to get licensed and take the Series 65 exam. The Series 65 is a comprehensive, 3-hour, 130-question exam that is required to be a registered investment advisor. The test consists of four parts: 1) Laws, Regulations, and Guidelines, Including Prohibition on Unethical Business Practices. 2) Client Investment Recommendations and Strategies 3) Investment Vehicle Characteristics and 4) Economic Factors and Business Information. To pass, you must get at least 94 questions correct for a passing score of 72%. You are required to be sponsored by a firm to be eligible to take the test. Once you are sponsored by a firm to take the test, you are eligible to sign up for the test with the Financial Industry Regulatory Authority, aka FINRA. The process of studying for the test was a long one; I began studying while I was playing in the Arizona Fall League in October and continued to study on a virtually daily basis until the day I passed the test in late January. The exam itself was extremely difficult. Of all the tests that I have ever taken (including the LSAT) this was by far the most difficult and the most stressful. The overall experience is one that I am thankful for. I certainly learned a lot of things that I didn't know before my months of studying, and I believe the test does a really good job of making sure you understand the broad range of content that is required of being an investment advisor."

I was very pleased to read, and it was very gracious of Perrin to acknowledge, the important part that Satya and I played in advancing his future career as a registered investment advisor.

Again, with positive thoughts flowing, that night I got the good news I had been hoping for. Perrin called to say he was promoted and invited to join the Triple-A Colorado Springs Sky Sox in the Pacific Coast League. So, after almost a month in extended spring training, despite voicing his strong opinions on the adverse conditions minor leaguers experience, Perrin was nevertheless moving forward again on his road to the show. Sometimes it's hard to understand the ways of the Baseball Gods.

I was eager to see Perrin pitch for the first time in Triple-A and booked travel arrangements to visit with him in Colorado Springs, a short hop, skip and a jump from Kansas City. However, for me, this was strictly a business trip. I was going as Perrin's boss representing Satya, hoping to attract future clients to my firm. I thought about how grateful I was to be at this new stage of my career, and how accurate Confucius was when he said, "Choose a job you love, and you will never have to work a day in your life."

On my forty-fourth birthday, I arranged my work schedule so I could attend a hot yoga class and get in thirty minutes of reflexology before I picked up Kayla and Nate from school. Later that night, after our celebratory birthday dinner out and everyone else asleep, I clicked on the MLB app on my iPhone to check in on Perrin's new team, the Colorado Springs Sky Sox. I did not expect to see Perrin on the mound on his first day on the roster, but to my surprise, Perrin had just come into the game to pitch.

The Baseball Gods have impeccable timing. They arranged Perrin's Triple-A debut against the Omaha Storm Chasers, the Triple-A affiliate of my Kansas City Royals! It occurred to me that if Dayton Moore, the General Manager of the Royals, and his scouts had not gotten a good look at Jon Perrin yet, they were about to get their chance for sure. Watching Perrin pitch for the first time in Triple-A was a thrill, and the fact that he was pitching against the Royals Triple-A farm team was simply the icing on my birthday cake. Perrin pitched well, and I went to sleep that night as happy for him as I could be, and a year older.

I assumed the Baseball Gods would appreciate it if the first thing I did when I arrived in Colorado Springs was to visit the Garden of the Gods. The Garden is a registered National Natural Landmark with dramatic views, 300-foot towering sandstone rock formations that rest against a backdrop of snow-capped mountains, easy and challenging hiking trails and, brilliant blue skies. I remembered my parents describing their visit here on vacation a few years prior, and I never forgot how they marveled about the park's sheer beauty, majestic rock structures and inspiring views.

After landing at the Colorado Springs Municipal Airport, I wasted no time beginning my spiritual pilgrimage. I got in my Enterprise rental car and headed straight for the legendary Garden of the Gods. As I drove, I was surprised to see that the Garden was not in some remote location like the Grand Canyon, or way out in the desert like Joshua Tree National Park. Rather, the Garden was almost hidden and nestled deep inside a canyon just outside of the city limits of Colorado Springs. As I approached the National Park, commercialized suburbia melted away in the warm sunshine and I quickly became immersed in the majestic Colorado wilderness. Once deep within the canyon, I no longer remembered the bustling town I had just left behind a few short miles back. I was too awestruck by the amazing scene of towering rock structures that looked like they were sculpted and placed there by the gods.

I parked the rental car and slowly began my walk through the garden of giant red rock formations. As I strolled, I felt a sense of awe and wondered how this garden could have been formed. Perhaps millions of years ago, this land was under water and these glorious red sandstone rock formations were slowly molded over time, sitting so peacefully in the most unique and glorious poses. When the high-water level finally receded, the giant rocks were left standing in these extraordinary positions. High above the garden, I saw huge cloud formations that looked like fluffy white pillows slowly drifted across the blue sky. Far away in the distance, I could see beautiful mountains reaching across the skyline covered with snow. My parents were right. The Garden of the Gods did not disappoint.

I immediately called my mom and dad to share my experience with them and confirm that they were correct. The Garden of the Gods was truly beautiful and a very special, spiritual place indeed. I remember my dad saying during our phone conversation that even an atheist who visited this place would come away convinced that this earth had to be created by God.

After the conversation with my parents, it seemed appropriate that I find a nice spot in this beautiful place to sit down in the shade, meditate, and give thanks. The sounds of nature were all around me. I could feel and hear the wind blow. I heard the birds chirping and singing. Occasionally, a couple would walk by and I could hear every word of their conversation while maintaining my meditative state. Yet, despite all the subtle distractions, I continued my breathing and remained focused on my mantra. During meditation, I repeated my "protection" mantra: "Spirit Guides, *Guardian* Angels, Ascended Masters, Higher Self, I thank you, I thank you, I thank you. Please protect me with everything I say, everything I do, and everywhere I go. Sat nam, namaste."

With the visit to the Garden of the Gods in my memory and rear-view mirror, I checked into my hotel, did some yoga and then headed to Security Service Field, the home of the Sky Sox, for the first of three Pacific Coast League games. Driving to the ballpark, I listened to Phish, my favorite jamband, on Spotify performing their Hampton/Winston-Salem, 1997 setlist. As I cruised down the highway, I enjoyed the view of Colorado's snowcapped mountains in the distance and jammed out to Phish songs "Run Like an Antelope," "My Soul," "Sparkle," "Fluffhead," and "Down with Disease." It was a nice ride.

The combination of Phish music and the beautiful topography reminded me of the great time I had in Colorado after turning 40. I met several of my college friends in Denver to see Phish play a three-night run at Dick's Sporting Goods Park, a Phish Labor Day weekend tradition. I'll never forget the first night when the band played a melodic, dream-like, 30-minute jam during the song "Simple." When Phish started to slowly jam out the song and move into uncharted territory, the music reached a special, magical place. I thought of it as "sonic bliss." Everything was just right. The sound quality, the lights, the smiles on the faces of everyone at the concert. Later in the concert, when Phish played another long jam, it felt as if the stadium had morphed into a mystical wonderland, all was well with the world, and I had seen a glimpse of an upcoming golden age.

I still love music, especially jambands like Phish, and plan to author books about the music industry in the future. However, my post-college music career days were now long gone. Instead of watching a three-night run of Phish concerts, I was catching a three-game series between the Omaha Storm Chasers and the Colorado Springs Sky Sox. But I had a strong feeling that my Baseball Gods adventures and my love of music would soon cross paths.

I arrived at the ballpark ahead of schedule. As I approached the will call line at the box office to pick up my ticket, I felt as if I had traveled back in time to the early 1900s. The music blasting through the stadium speakers was reminiscent of the "Roaring Twenties." In addition, there was a display of very well-maintained antique cars lined up in front of the stadium turnstiles. The cars reminded me of the old Model-T Fords and Buicks. Somehow, the vintage cars and the big band music also reminded me of the days of prohibition in New York City in the 1930s.

As I entered the stadium, I saw a few players warming up. Continuing with the nostalgia theme, they were all wearing "throw-back" uniforms. Several of the players were dressed in high socks and knicker pants. It turned out the Sky Sox organization was honoring their past that day and celebrating their future with a "Cheers to 45 More Years" campaign.

I was not aware that the city of Colorado Springs had such a rich baseball tradition. I learned that its first professional baseball team, the "Millionaires," was organized in 1901. An usher told me that the team got its name during the Colorado gold rush at the turn of the century, when many of the locals became millionaires. I also learned that the team left town in 1916 and the region was left without a local baseball team until the game's popularity boomed after World War II.

More than thirty years after the Millionaires departed, a new team finally arrived. In 1950, the Chicago White Sox planted a minor league team in Colorado Springs and named it the Sky Sox, a cute name for an affiliate owned by the White Sox in a location with the highest altitude in the country. Unfortunately, the team folded after the Western League went bankrupt. Local Colorado Springs baseball fans would have to wait another thirty years for another team to arrive.

In 1988, the Cleveland Indians organization arrived in Colorado Springs, associated with the minor league Triple-A Pacific Coast League, and management retained the Sky Sox name for the team. After five seasons affiliated with the Indians, the city of Denver was awarded a major league franchise for the 1993 baseball season, and that new expansion team, the Colorado Rockies, arranged for the Sky Sox to become its top minor league affiliate. Following the 2014 season, after more than a decade with the Rockies, the Sky Sox affiliation was reassigned to the Milwaukee Brewers.

The Pacific Coast League covers quite a lot of acreage, including the Midwest, the Southwest, and the Pacific coast of the United States. The Triple-A minor league teams that play in this league seem to find homes in medium-sized metropolitan areas across these parts of the country that are not big enough to support a major league team, but are far enough away from a major city so that they don't compete for fans. In 2018, the league included the Albuquerque Isotopes (Colorado Rockies), the Iowa Cubs (Chicago Cubs), the Fresno Grizzlies (Houston Astros), the Las Vegas 51s (New York Mets), the Nashville Sounds (Oakland Athletics), the El Paso Chihuahuas (San Diego Padres), the New Orleans Baby Cakes (Miami Marlins), the Oklahoma Dodgers (Los Angeles Dodgers), the Reno Aces (Arizona Diamondbacks), the Round Rock Express (Texas Rangers), the Sacramento River Cats (San Francisco Giants), the Salt Lake Bees (Los Angeles Angels), the Tacoma Rainiers (Seattle Marines), and, of course, the Omaha Storm Chasers (Kansas City Royals) and the Colorado Springs Sky Sox (Milwaukee Brewers). I think you get the idea here.

In my continuing quest to expand my knowledge of baseball, my research revealed that in 2017, more than 40 million fans attended minor league baseball games of more than 250 baseball teams across 20 minor and independent baseball leagues. Over the last decade, more than 70 million fans attended Pacific Coast League games. I concluded that I am not the only person who loves baseball and goes to minor league games.

At the ballpark, I started to read *The Inside Pitch*, the game day magazine of the Sky Sox, and learned that the President of the Pacific Coast League was a man named Branch B. Rickey, a name awfully familiar to me and all baseball historians. At first I thought this was a typo because the Branch Rickey I was familiar with was one of the most important people in baseball history, and, in my opinion, American history. Branch Rickey was the courageous team owner of the Brooklyn Dodgers who decided to break the color barrier in baseball and sign the first black player ever to a major league team. Branch Rickey signed the legendary Jackie Robinson! It turns out that Branch B. Rickey, the President of the Pacific Coast League, was, in fact, the grandson of that legendary former team owner of the Brooklyn Dodgers.

Reading on, I learned that not only did Branch Rickey, the grandpa, help pave the way for major social changes in America, he was also responsible for creating the framework for the modern-day minor league farm system. And members of his family have followed in his baseball footsteps. His son, Branch Rickey Jr., worked as a farm director for both the Brooklyn Dodgers and the Pittsburgh Pirates and the afore-mentioned Branch B. Rickey, the grandson, starting working in baseball in 1963 when he was only 17.

Putting *The Inside Pitch* aside and perusing the stadium, I realized that Security Service Field in Colorado Springs is bigger than MGM Park in Biloxi, where the Double-A Biloxi Shuckers play. It has a seating capacity of 8,500 compared to 6,076 for MGM Park. The size and layout of the field reminded me of the stadiums in the Cactus League in Arizona. The stadium sits right in the suburbs of Colorado Springs, adjacent to a community of single-family homes with a golf course. The field design is pretty straightforward and the outfield walls are symmetrical: 350 feet down the left and right field lines, 385 feet in the left and right-center, and 410 feet in deep, straight-away center field.

There is a new commercial space with shopping and restaurants just minutes away from the Security Service Field, including a Zoë's Kitchen. You may recall that it was at Zoë's in Overland Park, KS that Jon Perrin and I first met. We ate lunch at Zoë's for our first meal together. We agreed to meet up after the game for dinner, not at Zoë's, but at Tokyo Joe's, a new, casual fast food place that had just opened up right next door. It's just like Zoë's Kitchen, but serves Japanese cuisine.

At dinner that night, while Perrin and I were eating at Tokyo Joe's, I was able to hear music playing through the restaurant's speakers. To my surprise, the tune in the background was "When it Rains it Pours," a song belonging to my new favorite band, Twiddle. Twiddle, like Phish, is a band from Vermont, and both are very popular in Colorado. Twiddle, hoping to become as well-known and as successful as Phish, has sold out the Boulder Theater on more than one occasion and has also played at Colorado's legendary music venue, the Red Rocks Amphitheater.

I discovered Twiddle in the summer of 2016, when Phish keyboard player Page McConnell sat in with the band to play "When it Rains it Pours" at Tumble Down, the Twiddle music festival in Vermont. The song has a melodic and dramatic building jam that was perfect for McConnell to join in on. While the performance I watched on YouTube made me an instant Twiddle fan, it was the lyrics of the song that had the biggest impact on me. The song's chorus, sung by Twiddle lead singer Mihali Savoulidis, says "Awake now, listen to the words I'm saying in this line, that your life will be just fine and troubles do not stay, they get replaced with good times, now you got a great life, smile as you walk by, thinking about the day." These lyrics touched me deeply and made me realize that my midlife crisis was truly over. I realized that I was on the right path and, going forward, I would remain grateful, humble and happy.

This Friday night in April at Security Service Field was cold and windy, and the stadium was pretty empty. In the fourth inning, the Sky Sox brought in 16-year veteran and team leader Tim Dillard to pitch. Dillard quickly established his dominating presence. Standing at 6'5," with a thick, long beard that has become his iconic look, he is an imposing figure on the mound. On top of that, Dillard has a unique side-arm pitching windup, and after I saw his first pitch, he had my undivided attention. His pitches were coming up and in at an unusual angle, moving dynamically with wicked twists and turns, making it difficult for most batters who were seeing Dillard pitch for the first time. On this evening, Tim Dillard looked unhittable. In fact, he finished three complete innings without giving up a hit. Dillard's outing was a joy to watch.

Dillard's performance that night was particularly special because Security Service Field in the high altitude of Colorado Springs is well known as a hitter's ballpark. It is a venue notorious for lighting up pitchers with lots of hits and runs scored. But on this night, Dillard was clearly in the zone. At dinner with Perrin that night after the game, I raved about how impressive Dillard looked to me. As if the Baseball Gods were trying to get my attention, I subsequently learned a lot more about Tim Dillard.

Dillard is one of the funniest people on the planet. Off the baseball field, he often is seen wearing a wool hat with a cartoon logo of himself on the front and wearing colorful, usually orange, sunglasses. He has developed a cult-like following on social media for his hilarious antics off the field and in the team clubhouse. He is active on YouTube, Twitter and Instagram and frequently can be seen performing musical skits or movie parodies that he films and edits himself.

My favorite Tim Dillard moment is the comedy sketch video where he and a teammate lip synch to "Despacito," the popular Justin Bieber Latin music song.

Recently, Dillard was in the sports news because he started a baseball podcast with Ben Zobrist, his friend and a fellow ballplayer. Their friendship began shortly after their wives met in church. Zobrist played for the 2015 Kansas City Royals team that won the World Series, and the next season, he signed a free agent contract with the Chicago Cubs. The Cubs went on to win the 2016 World Series, their first in 108 years, and Zobrist was voted the series MVP. With back-to-back World Series victories with two different teams, the Baseball Gods must really love Ben Zobrist.

The next morning, I went for a walk on the golf course near my hotel and later did my daily yoga routine on the terrace of my hotel room. I was feeling great after my walk and workout and was inspired to go into full geek mode and visit the American Numismatic Association's Money Museum in downtown Colorado Springs. You may recall, I am a true "gold bug" and have carefully followed the precious metals market for many years as an integral part of my investment strategy at Satya. I enjoyed my visit to this very interesting museum, and even purchased some coins in its gift shop. However, it was something on the museum's façade that really caught my attention.

Outside on the wall of the museum, there were engraved pictures of the most influential people in the numismatic coin world. One engraving was of Raymond W. Dillard, a recipient of the Medal of Merit from the ANA. I saw the name Dillard and knew immediately that this was a message straight from the Baseball Gods. Based on what I already knew about Tim Dillard, and since I had thought about interviewing ballplayers for my book series, it occurred to me, right then and there, that the Sky Sox pitcher would be a really cool person to interview. Realizing that this was my chance, I asked Perrin to see if he could arrange it.

Like a closer coming into a game with two outs in the bottom of the ninth inning, up by one run, Perrin delivered. Perrin texted me that Dillard agreed to meet with me before the game on Sunday morning. I had bought a few silver coins at the money museum store the day before and decided to give one to Perrin and another to Dillard as a thank you for the interview.

While I was already looking forward to my Sunday interview with Dillard, the Baseball Gods had someone else they wanted me to talk to first. The Saturday ballgame had an early afternoon start, and even though the crowd was similar in size to that of night before, these fans sounded particularly energetic. Perhaps the sunny, warm weather had something to do with it, since it had been cold and windy the night before. I thought it was funny when the stadium announcer introduced the "Kiss Cam" segment between innings, usually a fan favorite, but the cameras could not locate any couples interested in kissing their partners. I've been to hundreds of ballgames and this was the first time ever that I had seen a Kiss Cam segment end without kisses. After several attempts to find willing participants, the announcer said, with disappointment and sarcasm in his voice, "Or just look at your cellphones."

During the game, I made my way over to right field and

noticed a setup of sophisticated sabermetric equipment. This was of particular interest to me because I had just read *The Only Rule Is It Has to Work* on my flight to Colorado, a book written by Ben Lindbergh and Sam Miller. This book is about an independent league team using sabermetrics to turn its ball club around based on advanced statistical analysis. The authors describe the initial difficulties in capturing the statistics they needed to analyze because the technological equipment at their team's stadium was inadequate. As I marveled at all the cameras and equipment set up here at Security Service Field, I realized how much technology has advanced, and could see first-hand its growing importance in the statistical world of baseball.

That wasn't the only thing that I saw in that right field corner. I noticed a female police officer standing right behind me, looking over my right shoulder. I turned to my right and joked with the officer that working a baseball game seemed like a pretty good gig to me. She replied that it was, because fans were usually orderly and respectful, but from time to time, she had to mix it up with some fans who may have had one or two beers too many.

We got to talking and the next thing I knew, I was telling the police officer about my visit to the AMA Museum and receiving my first gold coin as a gift from Reggie's grandmother. For some reason, I felt compelled to mentioned the Devinki family Holocaust story of survival, and when I did, it was as if a light turned on deep inside her soul. The police officer, who had listened intently to my story, had her own story to tell as well.

Her name was Aaron Walker and she told me that she was a second generation American. Her grandmother, like Reggie's, was born in Poland. The Walkers were Christian, not Jewish. Her grandmother's family lived on the outskirts of the city of Warsaw. When the Nazi tanks rolled into their small town, everyone was rounded up, put on trains, and taken to the concentration camps, Jews and non-Jews alike. While most Jews were later redirected to death camps rather than work camps, Officer Walker's grandmother spent the next few years of her life working and living in Auschwitz, perhaps the most infamous concentration camp of all.

At the end of the war, the Russian army arrived in Poland and liberated many people from Nazi concentration camps. When they entered Auschwitz, Officer Walker's grandmother was finally freed. Like Reggie's grandparents, Officer Walker's family immigrated to the United States after the war and settled in a town between Washington D.C. and Baltimore. Aaron's father grew up a proud and patriotic American and, after graduating from college, got a job working for the Department of Homeland Security. Growing up with a father working in law enforcement inspired Officer Walker to follow a similar career path.

Just after Officer Walker finished her captivating family story, a towering foul ball was hit our way. It had a vertical trajectory on the way up and came crashing down right behind us into a stack of boxes and a garbage can stationed behind a soda and beer vendor. I ran over to try and get the ball as a souvenir for Nate. When the drink vendor picked up the ball, I yelled, "Hey, can I have that ball so I can give it to my son?" The vendor looked at me, and with an apologetic look on her face, tossed it to the man in front of the line buying drinks. The man caught the vendor's toss and then turned and tossed the ball to me, with a smile on his face. I thanked the man, turned to Officer Walker, and said with joyful amazement, "The Baseball Gods are Real."

CHAPTER NINE

The Veteran

"Yeah, I was in the show. I was in the show for 21 days once—
the 21 greatest days of my life."
—Crash Davis, *Bull Durham*

TIM DILLARD HAS A CULT-LIKE FOLLOWING IN THE
baseball world for his long career, hilarious YouTube videos,
clubhouse leadership, and unique sidearm pitching style. He
has more than forty thousand Instagram and Twitter followers, and his fans love the hysterical videos he produces that
chronical the hard life in the minor leagues. For all of these
reasons, you can find many Dillard admirers on the internet through social media and in person at the ballpark at his
minor league games.

It was at one such minor league game, my third at Security
Service Field, that I saw a group of Brewers fans who had
flown into town for the game all wearing Tim Dillard look-
alike costumes. These outfits included big black beards, orange
sunglasses and Tim Dillard branded T-shirts. These loyal fans,
who no doubt traveled some distance to get here, went crazy

when they got Dillard's attention by yelling out, "Dilly Dilly." The phrase, Dilly Dilly, became very popular for a period of time because of its use in a successful television commercial by Budweiser in its Medieval Bud Light Beer Campaign. Given Tim's last name, the catch phrase was perfect.

I was really looking forward to my interview with Dillard, and pleased that Jon Perrin was able to arrange it on such short notice. With a pro career spanning 16 years, albeit most of it traveling in the minor leagues, Dillard arguably had seen it all on and off the baseball field. I was hoping he might have some great stories to share about the Baseball Gods. Despite Dillard's long career and popularity, many baseball fans might not know that he is a man of faith, a fact that made interviewing him even more interesting.

Dillard's baseball journey probably began even before he was born. Dillard's father, Steve, was a professional baseball player, a second baseman, who played in the major leagues between 1975 and 1982 for four different teams. He made it to the show in 1975 with the Boston Red Sox. After retiring from baseball, Steve Dillard managed in the minor leagues, and later became an infield instructor with the Houston Astros. Tim Dillard followed in his father's baseball footsteps, but as a pitcher rather than as a second baseman.

Dillard, the son, was born in 1983 and learned to play baseball in Little League and by watching his dad in the pros. He was first drafted by the Milwaukee Brewers in 2001 as the 448th pick in the 15th round. Dillard did not sign with the team at that time and decided instead to attend community college to further his education. Perhaps it was his destiny that he play for the Brewers because they selected Dillard again in the 2002 draft. This time Dillard, chosen in the 34th round as the 1,009th pick, signed a professional baseball contract and began his road to the show at the bottom of the minor league system.

Dillard's first stop as a minor league rookie was in Montana with the Helena Brewers. His career got off to a solid start, pitching both as a starter and as a reliever. Next stop for Dillard was in Wisconsin where he joined the Class-A Beloit Snappers in 2004. Not spectacular there, he had a 2-5 win-loss record with a 3.94 ERA. Playing for the Snappers, however, Dillard did show that he could potentially be a solid closer by recording ten saves. At his next stop the following season, in warmer weather in Florida with the Class-A Advanced Brevard County Manatees, Dillard had his breakout year, not as a closer, but as a starting pitcher. There he made 28 starts, went 12-10 and had an ERA of 2.48, the lowest in his young career. He also pitched the most innings in the league and recorded 128 strikeouts. Dillard's performance was noticed, earning him a spot on the Florida State League Postseason All-Star team, and at the conclusion of the 2005 season, he was named the Brewers Minor League Pitcher of the Year.

After gaining some career momentum in Florida, Dillard was promoted and moved a little further north to Alabama to join the Double-A Huntsville Stars. Dillard had another solid season there making twenty-five starts, four relief appearances, and finishing the year with a 10-7 record and a 3.26 ERA. He led his team in wins, starts, and innings pitched, and came in second in strikeouts. Dillard was recognized for his efforts and was selected to the Southern League Mid-Season All-Star game. With successful back-to-back seasons in Single-A and then Double-A, Dillard earned another promotion, this time to Triple-A.

Continuing his journey north in the minors the next season, Dillard adjusted well to Tennessee playing for the Nashville Sounds in Triple-A. There he had an 8-4 record and 4.74 ERA in 34 games with 16 starts. Dillard returned to the Nashville Sounds for a second season in 2008, but he didn't stay long.

On May 23, 2008, a date Dillard will always remember, he received the news that every ball player fantasizes about from the time he first steps on to a ballfield. Dillard got called up to the show by the Milwaukee Brewers. He had finally made it to the major leagues. On the same day that he received this exciting news, Dillard made his major league debut. Living his life-long dream, he pitched one inning that night and recorded his first major league strikeout.

For the next four years, Dillard continued to live the dream playing baseball in the show. As a relief pitcher coming out of the bullpen for the Brewers, he made 13 appearances in 2008, 24 in 2009, 24 again in 2011 and 34 in 2012. One year, Dillard even got the opportunity to join the Brewers in the post-season playoffs.

During this five-year period, Dillard's dream of pitching in the big leagues was interrupted twice. First, during the 2010 season, he was optioned back to the minor leagues and rejoined the Triple-A Nashville Sounds. Dillard was promoted to the show again in 2011, but this stint was short-lived. In 2012, he was sent back down to Nashville, but unlike his previous demotion, this time he did not get called back up. At this point, Dillard's career seemed to go into a tailspin. By 2014, Dillard found himself in Pennsylvania in the Atlantic League of independent baseball pitching for the Lancaster Barnstormers, and shortly thereafter in the Mexican Baseball League.

Dillard had reached a point in his career where most ball-players would have simply given up. He was now over 30, hadn't been to the show in three years, and no major league team wanted his services. Yet, he chose not to abandon his baseball dreams. Instead, Dillard continued to work hard at his trade, developed a keen sense of humor, and believed his faith in God would help him get back on track. His sheer will, determination and faith paid off because Dillard was re-signed by the Brewers in 2015 and has played for their Triple-A Colorado Springs Sky Sox affiliate ever since.

With Tim Dillard still on my mind, I met Perrin that night for dinner and we chatted about baseball, Satya and the next day's interview. Then I went back to my hotel room where I did a yoga session and meditated on the back terrace, taking in another beautiful Colorado evening sky. I emerged from meditation with a flurry of insightful questions to ask Dillard. One by one they came to me, like a massive data transmission from another dimension, and I typed them into my iPhone as quickly as I could. When the flurry ceased, I decided to whittle the questions down to ten, and sent them to Perrin for his review and blessing. Then I called and spoke with Reggie and the kids, as I do every night I'm away from home, and told them what was going on here.

Despite my excitement, I slept well that night. I did morning yoga on my last full day in Colorado, and then left my hotel to meet Perrin and Dillard outside the clubhouse as we had previously arranged. When I arrived at the entrance to the clubhouse, Perrin and Dillard were awaiting my arrival. There

they were, these two baseball pitchers, standing tall, looking like twin towers to me. Perrin stands at 6'5" and Dillard
appears even taller, with a much broader frame. I guess if they
played on the same basketball team, they would be difficult to
beat, blocking shots and dunking all over the competition. We
shook hands and exchanged greetings.

I broke the ice by asking Perrin if he had seen Pablo Sandoval
on TV the night before. Sandoval, you may recall, was the
third baseman who caught the last out in Game 7 of the 2014
World Series at Kauffman Stadium when the San Francisco
Giants defeated my Kansas City Royals. He also happened to
be the first batter Perrin faced when he toed the mound for the
first time in the Cactus League during spring training. During
last night's game on TV, the Giants had depleted their pitching staff so they brought in Sandoval to pitch the ninth inning.
In a 15-6 loss against the Los Angeles Dodgers, he threw eleven
pitches, eight of them strikes, and got three outs. It was a
classic 1-2-3 perfect inning. The three of us laughed at how
awesome that was for a non-pitcher.

After Dillard and I said goodbye to Perrin, we walked looking for a place for our interview. As we strolled, I mentioned
that he looked great pitching on Friday night, almost unhittable. Dillard laughed and replied with a humble response,
deflecting my praise, "Sometimes it works, and sometimes it
doesn't." We found a table on a patio overlooking the baseball
diamond at Security Service Field, and while the groundskeep-
ers groomed the infield and players started their morning
warm-ups, Dillard and I began the interview. I was curious
and asked him if knew anything about me. Dillard said he
knew that I was a fan of his and a friend of Perrin's. I took this

opportunity to briefly explain how Perrin and I met, became friends, and eventually became colleagues. I told Dillard that I was also an author with a love of baseball, summarized my first book, and explained that I was interested in featuring him in my second book.

My first question for Dillard related to his relationship with Ben Zobrist, his co-host on their podcast *SHOW and GO*, and how they became friends. In response, Dillard talked about his promotion to Triple-A, followed by his move to Nashville with his wife and family, and their search to find a church that was a good fit for the Dillard family. The second church they visited felt right to them and they joined. Right away, Dillard's wife was introduced to Zobrist's. I told Tim that I had read in an article that their wives first met in church, and his story confirmed it. The Dillard's and the Zobrist's have been great friends ever since, and they even live close to each other in the offseason in Nashville. I asked Dillard if he thought that this meeting in church was a coincidence or preordained. He said he believed it was divine providence.

Continuing our conversation, I was surprised to learn that, unlike many baseball players and athletes in other sports, Dillard was not superstitious. Nor did he believe in karma. I asked if he subscribed to the theory "what goes around comes around," which I suggested may be karma but stated somewhat differently. Dillard didn't think so and said that he felt that life, and things that happen in the world, are too random and unpredictable to be karma. Staying on the subject, I offered up a few examples that, over time, have convinced me that karma does exist, and that what goes around does come around, but Dillard could not be swayed.

Based on our conversation about superstition and karma, I was not surprised when Dillard told me that he was not a fan of baseball rituals either. He joked about players who honestly believed that they had to follow the same exact routine every day. He explained that once a player gets called up to the show, everything is different, including the locker room, the food, the travel, and even the schedule. The previous routine that a person might have followed for good luck was now out the window. He ridiculed baseball superstitions, like the one in the movie *Bull Durham* where a player uses rosary beads to pray over his bat for good luck. He said jokingly, "Where are all those ballplayers now? They are all gone, out of the game, so obviously their superstitious practices did not help them." Dillard explained that while he is an optimistic person, it is his view that the power of positive thinking is useless. He believes that a player has little control over his own destiny, thereby rebutting certain theories like the law of attraction, a new age belief system whereby people can manifest their desired reality with thoughts, attitudes and behaviors. He certainly didn't embrace my theory that the Baseball Gods are real.

Dillard gave me an example of his own. He asked me to imagine that I was a pitcher on the mound who did everything right, from my preparation to my pre-game routine, and did all of my other superstition stuff. When you make your first pitch, he continued, you realize that what happens next is out of your control. For example, the umpire has a narrow strike zone that day and your strikes are called balls. Or you throw a good pitch that gets the batter to hit a ground ball, but the second baseman makes an error. Or you may be pitching here, in the high altitude of Colorado Springs on any day of the week, and the ball just flies out of the park, even though you threw a good pitch. Although I had a different view on the subject, I had to admit that Dillard made some really good points of his own.

Agreeing to disagree, I decided to go with the flow and move the interview in another direction. I asked Dillard the extent to which he thought that pitching in Colorado might have hurt his statistics and hindered his career. I gave an example of former Sky Sox hurler Stephen Kohlscheen, whose pitching statistics were dramatically better in away games than at home in Colorado Springs. When I said that name, Dillard smiled and replied, "Yeah, I know Kohlscheen." I pondered out loud, if Kohlsheen's career may have gone differently if he had played his Triple-A ball someplace else, and wondered, to myself, the same about Dillard.

Dillard acknowledged that playing in Colorado may have hurt his career, but then asked, "How do you measure success?" Dillard explained that he used to think that success was all about playing in the major leagues. However, now, as a more mature and thoughtful person, he judges success by the impact he has on other people's lives. Dillard has affection for every person he comes across and enters the clubhouse every-day thinking about who and how he can help. As the team leader of the Sky Sox, Dillard gets to guide many baseball players as they move up and down the baseball ranks and pass through Triple-A on their road to and from the show.

Whether he believes in them or not, I think the Baseball Gods are proud of Tim Dillard and his approach to baseball, and to life in general. I think they are on his side. At that point, I hoped he would get another chance to go to the show in 2019.

Spoiler alert - after 16 seasons with the same major league team, the Milwaukee Brewers, Dillard signed a contract with the Texas Rangers for the 2019 season.

After answering many of the questions I had prepared for the interview, it was time for Dillard to leave for practice. I thanked him for his time and told him that if our interview makes it into my next book, I would send him a draft for his review before publication. I also gave him his gift, a US Silver Eagle coin with a Mark Twain design on it that I had purchased the day before at the Money Museum. I told him that not only was Mark Twain one of the most well-known authors of all time, he was also a humorist, and one of the funniest people of all time. Having gotten to know Dillard, I felt that the coin was an appropriate gift for me to give to him. We shook hands, I thanked Dillard again for the interview, and thought to myself, Tim Dillard, may the Baseball Gods always be with you, even if you are not a believer.

CHAPTER TEN

The Vegan

"If slaughterhouses had glass walls,
everyone would be a vegetarian."
—Paul McCartney

WHEN MY FAMILY AND I MOVED FROM ARMONK, NY in Westchester County to Leawood, KS in 2012, I was a carnivore. Red meat was an essential part of my diet and I probably ate it on average four days a week. In Kansas City, famous for barbeque, this pattern continued. In fact, there was a period during which I ate lunch at Oklahoma Joes, a very popular barbeque joint near my home, several times a week. Oklahoma Joes is so well known that it sells its special barbeque sauce online worldwide. This situation did not help my waistline and, during this period of time, I put on weight, my cholesterol level rose dramatically, and my blood pressure increased.

That's why, just before my 40th birthday, I gave up red meat. At a hot yoga class at Core Energy in Overland Park, while holding my downward facing dog position, with sweat dripping from my forehead onto the yoga mat, I finally accepted what doctors and nutritionists had been saying for decades. Red meat is not good for me or my heart, and it causes inflammation in my body.

Right after that class, I sat in my car, still covered in sweat, and googled on my iPhone the correlation between red meat and inflammation. The evidence I found was compelling and well documented. Next, to reconfirm my decision to go without red meat, I searched the health benefits of doing so. I learned that avoiding red meat could help ease the joint pain in my fingers and hands, since arthritis manifests itself as inflammation in the body. I stopped eating red meat that day and have never looked back. My promise, no more hamburgers at fast food restaurants, no more hot dogs at the ballpark, and most painfully, no more Kansas City barbeque, not even at Oklahoma Joes.

I knew it was time for this dramatic change in my eating habits, and that the change would be good for me. And it was. Over the next several months, I lost weight, my cholesterol level came down, and I was, in general, feeling better, healthier. Even though I had given up red meat, I still ate turkey, chicken, pork and fish. That too would soon change.

Months later, we received an invitation to attend the wedding of Karen and Jordan Lerner, Reggie's cousins, in Toronto. Fortunately, we were able to go. We enjoyed a wonderful weekend in one of Canada's truly beautiful cities. Our sight-seeing visit to the top of the CN Tower was truly a highlight, as was Karen and Jordan's wedding.

While sight-seeing in Toronto, we traveled mostly using the subway system and noticed that each station had vegan advertisements plastered all over the walls. The anti-meat print ad campaign very cleverly compared pigs to dogs and, to make the ads even more effective, showcased puppies. One sign read, "Did you know that a baby pig is smarter than a dog?" Another ad showed a picture of an adorable puppy right next to an equally adorable baby pig. The top of the ad said, "What's the difference?" As an owner of two dogs, I had to admit, the point of the ad was clearly made.

When we returned to our hotel, a synchronicity occurred that was just incredible. Nate turned on the TV and found a *Simpsons* episode featuring the famous Beatle, Sir Paul McCartney, known to be a vegetarian. In this very funny episode, Homer Simpson's super-intelligent and thoughtful daughter, Lisa, becomes a vegetarian. Although a cartoon, the writers and producers of the *Simpsons* often use the show as a vehicle for serious discourse on current issues and events. In this instance, I watched Lisa Simpson awaken to vegetarianism and I found myself reacting the same way.

Nate, Kayla, and I watched the *Simpsons* episode together and, by the time the show was over, I just knew it was time for me to make another beneficial change in my diet. And that day, in my hotel room, in Toronto Canada, I became a vegetarian. The next day on Twitter I saw a quote from, you guessed it, Paul McCartney, which read, "If slaughterhouses had glass walls, everyone would be a vegetarian."

Watching that *Simpsons* episode had a big impact on me, and it might have started an awakening in my children. About a year later, after I became a vegetarian, Nate voluntarily stopped eating red meat. I was surprised, to say the least. A few months after that, Kayla made a big change in her diet as well.

During her summer vacation in 2016, Kayla was invited to spend a week with my parents in Armonk as she had done several times before. After another exhausting day sight-seeing in New York City with my folks, she would sometimes relax in bed at night and watch YouTube videos and Netflix documentaries on her iPad. Often, she would focus on videos and documentaries related to nutrition, like *Forks over Knives*. She learned that veganism is animal friendly and that a well-balanced, plant-based diet leads to good health and general well-being.

When Kayla returned to Kansas City from her vacation in New York, she was completely transformed. As a result of her research, she told Reggie and me that she had decided to skip over becoming a vegetarian and was going straight to vegan.

Kayla has become a diligent vegan and, thanks to the internet, extremely knowledgeable about how to maintain a healthy, balanced, plant-based diet. She has even met with a local nutritionist to be certain that she does it right, including making sure to get enough protein. Kayla taught herself how to prepare and cook all of her own meals, breakfast, lunch and dinner. My daughter inspired me, and she is responsible for paving the way for me to go from vegetarian to vegan.

When I advanced from vegetarianism to veganism, I noticed even more positive changes in my life. First, I lost more weight. When I looked in the mirror, I could see the difference in the shape of my body. I felt and looked healthier and more fit, boosting my happiness and self-confidence. The next thing I noticed was the reduction in my arthritis pain level and my psoriasis condition improved.

Switching to a vegan diet also changed my thoughts

regarding eating animals and I developed an even deeper empathy for them. Now I find it difficult to watch advertisements by steak restaurants that brag about how juicy and delicious their meats taste. Typically, these commercials flash slow motion video of raw meat on a grill, with seasonings being tossed about in the air as the animal flesh gets flipped over from one side to the other. When the raw meat hits the burning hot grill, it sizzles. These days, as far as food goes, I perceive pigs, chickens, and cows no differently than dogs. All of these animals have moms and dads, and sisters and brothers. All possess a certain level of intelligence and can express empathy. All are capable of loving and being loved. Turning vegan clearly has reshaped my perspective on this subject.

You might be surprised to learn that some of the world's best athletes have gone vegan. For example, some of the Ultimate Fighting Championship's most well-known fighters have done so. In Kenny Herzog's article "Why UFC's Toughest Fighters Are Going Vegan," he describes UFC commentator Joe Rogan's post-fight interview with Nate Diaz. Diaz had just defeated UFC Featherweight Champion Conor McGregor, one of the toughest guys in the world, in a bruising battle. During the interview after the fight, Diaz, who strictly abstains from meat, poultry and dairy, boasts "Who's the real caveman here? Who's the real beast? If anything, meat's gonna slow you down."

Veganism is gaining popularity in another tough guy sport too, football. At the end of the 2017 season, my Kansas City Chiefs suffered another heartbreaking playoff loss. This time, the Chiefs lost at home to the Tennessee Titans. The Chiefs, who had built up an early 21-3 lead, started losing steam in the fourth quarter while the Titans continued to fight on with increasing vigor. The Titans rallied to win the game 22-21, earning their first playoff win in 14 years. It turns out that almost a dozen members of the Titans were vegans. Most of them play on the defense, so let's take a closer look.

In 2017 the Titans defense ranked 3rd in the National Football League against the run and 5th in the league with a total of 40 quarterback sacks. Titans team leader in sacks with 5 was Wesley Woodyard, a vegan. Regarding his vegan diet, Woodyard told Luke Darby in his 2015 *GQ* article "The Real-Life Diet of a Vegan NFL Defensive Lineman," "My energy level's gone up…And it's just putting in good fuel to your body. And of course, it's always hard to keep weight on this time of the season. But it's worth it for me staying on top of my health."

Another popular football player, Chicago Bears defensive lineman David Carter, switched to a 100% plant-based diet in 2014. A typical vegan-day menu for Carter might include oatmeal with hemp protein, bananas and berries for breakfast, brown rice and black beans topped with avocado and cashew cheese for lunch, couscous with onion and garlic, and spinach salad with bell peppers for dinner. According to his interview with *GQ* magazine, Carter tries to eat 1.2 pounds of protein per day in the offseason. He eats 10,000 calories in a normal day, which includes 5 meals and a number of snacks. Carter is now a vegan activist, touting its benefits to all who will listen.

Some nutritionists believe that veganism, in addition to increasing stamina and energy on the playing field, may also lead to career longevity. At 40 years old, we saw New England Patriots quarterback Tom Brady play again in the Super Bowl to end the 2018 NFL season. What is the secret to his success? According to Dan Pompei of Bleacher Report, Brady embraces a unique "body work" approach to fitness that focuses more on the use of rubber resistance bands for high-intensity workouts rather than on power and strength workouts. However, perhaps the real secret to Brady's success and long career is something else. Maybe it's the fact that he carefully adheres to a vegan diet most of the year. I suspect only the "Football Gods" know the answer for sure.

In addition to the boxing ring and the football field, the vegan trend has reached the hardwood courts of the National Basketball Association. To cut weight and increase energy levels, an increasing number of NBA basketball players are embracing a vegan diet. I first learned about this from my friend and first guru, Eric Milano, who sent me a video of NBA legend John Salley talking about the benefits of eating vegan foods. NBA players who have gone vegan include Jahlil Okafor, Kyrie Irving, Damian Lillard, Enes Kanter, Wilson Chandler, JaVale McGee, Al Jefferson, Victor Oladipo and Michael Porter, Jr. It will be even more fun to watch the careers of these players now that I know they are vegans.

As the players on sports franchises worldwide start switching to better, higher quality plant-based food, they may also find their results on the field improve. An example of this can been seen across the pond in the English Football League. In 2014, the Forest Green Rovers, a mid-level English soccer team, became the first soccer club to go all-vegan. The players eat healthy vegan meals provided by the organization on a daily basis, and so do the fans in the stands. If they crave a hamburger, they have to settle for a veggie burger instead. A big salute to team owner and chairman, Dale Vince, for his vision. Some FGR fans have even become vegetarians away from the field since the club took meat off the stadium menu, and Mr. Vince knows that he is helping change people's lives in a positive way. This past season, FGR earned a promotion and now play in League Two English Football for the first time ever. Perhaps the team's success on the soccer field is a result of their players eating a healthy vegan diet.

The tale of tennis star Novak Djokovic is also on point. He was already a great player but was unable to break through the spell that Roger Federer and Raphael Nadal held over him. That is, until he went vegan, which he did for both ethical and health reasons. After he did so, Djokovic was in the best shape of his career, with an increase in stamina needed to excel in grueling 5-set matches at major championships. Djokovic went on to win several majors, a total of 16, behind only Federer and Nadal with 20 and 18, respectively, and is currently ranked #1 in the world. He attributes much of his success to his vegan diet. He and his wife, Jelena, even own a vegan restaurant in Monte Carlo.

Veganism has been shown to help athletes in the UFC, in the NFL, in the NBA, in soccer, and in tennis to improve their performance and extend careers. Not surprisingly, there are also vegan trailblazers in Major League Baseball. The first breeze of the winds of change started during the 2007 offseason when Prince Fielder, the 265-pound power hitting first baseman of the Milwaukee Brewers, decided to give up eating meat after he learned how animals were treated by the food industry. Fielder said that he "was totally grossed out" by the situation.

The breeze of change got stronger the next year. Like the legendary home run hitter Babe Ruth, Fielder was overweight. But unlike the beloved Babe, Fielder was actually heckled by fans because of his size. In the *New York Times* article entitled "Meat is Out at Fielder's Plate," written by Alan Schwarz, Fielder is quoted saying, "Fans last year were yelling at me, hey Prince, eat a salad!" Perhaps the Baseball Gods were trying to communicate with Fielder and were using the fans as the conduit to get his attention.

Maybe the Baseball Gods were using multiple approaches to get Fielder to make a change, first by making him aware of animal cruelty in the food industry, and then by having the fans taunt him about his weight. Whatever the reason, in the clubhouse of the Milwaukee Brewers, their star and home-run-hitting first baseman, Prince Fielder, decided to switch his diet and became the first and, at that time, the only self-proclaimed vegetarian in major league baseball.

Fielder got his protein from beans and shakes rather than from meat. Many skeptics declared that his energy level and hitting power would decrease. However, according to his *New York Times* article, Schwarz believed Fielder had all of the energy and power he always had, possibly more. For this article, Schwarz interviewed nutritional consultant Leslie Bonci of the University of Pittsburgh Medical Center. Bonci said convincingly, "Muscles cannot tell the difference between the protein found in soy burgers and poultry." Point made.

I wondered if the Baseball Gods were making a statement by having the first vegetarian in baseball history play for the Milwaukee Brewers. Wisconsin sports fans are notoriously famous for tailgating and cooking bratwurst. The Schwarz article even mentions that consuming meat is so engrained in Wisconsin culture that during Brewers games, eating contests featuring different varieties of wiener products are held in between innings.

By 2014, the eating habits of professional baseball players began to shift in earnest. Vicki Salemi's article "What MLB Players Really Eat." captured this trend and the change in baseball players' diets stating "Some rock out to veggies." Ballplayers were slowly making the transition, as did Matt Belisle, at the time a right-handed pitcher with the Colorado Rockies, who told Salemi that "his go-to take-out dish" was vegetarian Thai fried rice. By 2015, more and more baseball players began to realize that healthy eating habits might actually give them a competitive edge. And in 2016, healthy eating proved to be a team's secret weapon in helping them win a World Series championship.

Chicago Cubs star right-handed pitcher Jake Arrieta made changes to his diet in 2015 thinking doing so would make him an even more effective on the mound. Arrieta arrived at the Cubs' spring training facility in Mesa, Arizona with a new routine, one that included kale juice! In Mark Gonzales' 2015 *Chicago Tribune* article, "Cubs' Jake Arrieta Believes Healthier Diet Will Pay Off During Season," Arrieta said, "I try to start every day with some sort of vegetable and fruit juice before I eat any kind of solid food. Because that really jump starts your body and digestive system with the high content of micronutrients that your body needs." While Arrieta did still eat meat, he replaced red meat with lean chicken and seafood, which he said he eats only once or twice a week. He eats mostly fruits and vegetables on his new diet.

With his new diet in place, Arrieta had his best season ever in the major leagues that year. He had an amazing 22-6 won-loss record, with a 1.77 ERA, and received the Cy Young Award as the best pitcher in the National League. The next season in 2016, Arrieta had another great year, ending up with an 18-8 won-loss record. That was the year the Cubs won the World Series, their first championship since 1908. The city of Chicago went wild.

I should point out that the Cubs also had a great manager at the time, Joe Madden, who introduced pilates, yoga and meditation to the Cubs daily routine. Only the Baseball Gods know for sure whether it was the Cubs' manager, their new exercise program, or the change in Jake Arrieta's eating habits that made the difference in the fortunes of the Cubs' franchise.

The vegan trend that began in 2007 with Prince Fielder on the field kicked into high gear in 2017 off the field. That year, on opening day at Kauffman Stadium, I noticed a veggie burger and a veggie hotdog on the concession's menu for the first time. I was pleasantly surprised to see these new items and I felt that I may have manifested the change because it was something I had thought about in the past. The K even opened a kosher hotdog stand that served terrific potato knishes with spicy brown mustard, a classic staple at New York City kosher delicatessens. As a vegan, I loved those knishes, but passed on the hotdogs.

The Kansas City Royals were not the only team to serve vegan friendly offerings to their fans that year. Vegan friendly ballparks had really become a prime-time thing. For example, Citizens Bank Park, the Phillies home field in Philadelphia, sold veggie hot dogs, veggie soft tacos, farmer's market grain bowls, three-bean chili, and Bavarian pretzels. Over at AT&T

Park, the Giants ballpark in San Francisco, fans could now enjoy vegan franks and burgers, Cha-Cha bowls with fresh veggies and pineapple salsa, vegan tacos and burritos. Oriole Park, at Camden Yards in Baltimore, offered veggie wraps. Yankee Stadium not only offered vegan franks and black bean burgers, now vegan chili and veggie sushi were also available at concession stands. Citi Field, the home of the NY Mets, served up vegan pizza slices and potato knishes, in addition to vegan hotdogs and burgers. Dodgers Stadium deserved credit for offering Vietnamese noodle salad and sushi wraps. Target Field, home to the Minnesota Twins, gets it right by offering vegan brats and sausages. Globe Life Park, home to the Texas Rangers in Arlington, Texas, sold some of my personal favorites, vegan food brands known as Beyond Beef and Beyond Chicken. Fans in Arlington could now enjoy Texas barbeque with meat-free jerky. Oakland-Alameda County Coliseum received a special honorable mention from me for having an all-vegan food truck that served fake meat that tastes like the real thing. The truck served fried "chicken" strips and ground "beef," without the chicken or the beef.

The acceptance of this developing food trend by baseball management became official in my mind when the Pittsburgh Pirates dedicated an entire night to veganism. The Pirates hosted a "vegan night" on September 26, 2017, when the Baltimore Orioles were visiting PNC Park. Management appropriately named the event "Veggin' Out at the Ballpark!" Just as "Yoga Day at the Ballpark" caught on with fans across America, I hope that vegan night becomes a popular annual event at ballparks as well.

Last year I had my first veggie dog at Dodger Stadium during the 2018 National League Championship Series, and it was pretty darn good! I predict that as vegan foods, like my vegan Dodger dog and the "fake chicken" and "fake beef" sold at the Oakland-Alameda County Coliseum, become more popular and in greater demand, they will taste as good as or even better than the real thing, and a new mega health food trend will begin in this country. In a few years, we may see tailgaters across the land grilling before games as they always did, but with Gardein Chicken Fingers, Beyond Chicken Sandwiches and Impossible Burgers above the charcoal.

While Kaufman Stadium does not yet sponsor a vegan night, they do offer veggie hot dogs and veggie burgers as I previously mentioned. This came in handy a few days after I returned to Kansas City from my trip to visit Jon Perrin in Colorado Springs. I was home in time to join Nate and his fifth-grade elementary school class for a wonderful tradition called "School Day at the K." At School Day, the kids learn about weather and science in the morning, have a cookout lunch in the parking lot, and then watch the Royals play a day game in the afternoon.

At the cookout, the only foods served for lunch were beef hamburgers and beef hotdogs. Luckily for me, Kauffman Stadium now had vegetarian offerings. Before Nate and I left the stadium to attend the cookout, I was grateful that I could buy a veggie burger and fries to take with me to the parking lot. Perhaps next year, after some of the parents of Nate's classmates have read this book, Beyond Burgers will be added to the menu at the annual School Day at the K cookout. Even better, maybe they will be served in Nate's school cafeteria. You never know, they could be a big hit.

I should point out that despite the progress veganism has made in major league baseball, in other sports, and in ball-parks across the country, it has not yet found its way to the minor leagues, where the baseball world has dragged its feet. Jon Perrin tells me that he and his minor league teammates are often served fried chicken tenders and hot dogs for their pre-game dinner. Perrin once posted a photo on Instagram of the pre-game dinner offerings and wrote "Hot dogs and chicken fingers for pre-game spread...My life is a joke. #FuelThatFerrari." So, when it comes to serving healthier food to minor leaguer ballplayers, the Baseball Gods still have a lot of work to do.

CHAPTER ELEVEN

The Cemetery Run

"Let your mind rest easy, sleep well my friend. It's only our bodies that betray us in the end."

—Bruce Springsteen, from the song "We are Alive"

IN THE FIRST BOOK IN MY THE BASEBALL GODS ARE REAL series, I describe my first Akashic record session with energy worker Samantha Willis. Channeling through Samantha, my spirit guides predicted that I would have a spiritual transformation and share the changes in my life with the world. My *guardian* angels also predicted that old friends from my past would unexpectedly visit me in Kansas City to witness my transformation. This session proved to be prophetic.

First, my dear friend from early childhood, Seth Kornbluth, contacted me to say that he was coming to Kansas City on a business trip. Seth went to law school after graduating from college and now works as an attorney in the mortgage department of a large bank. As part of his job, he often travels from his New York City office to visit local banks and law firms in far off places like Overland Park, KS. Knowing that Seth was coming, I asked Reggie's Aunt Karen and Uncle Steve, who are Royals season ticket holders, if they had two extra seats for a ballgame the night Seth would be in town. They said they did and I was welcome to have them.

I picked Seth up at his hotel and we chatted during the 20-minute drive from downtown Kansas City to Kauffman Stadium. We parked, entered the stadium, and headed straight to Karen and Steve's great seats right along the rail near the dugout on the third base side of the field. Since we had not seen each other in more than a decade, Seth and I spent most of the first hour at the ballgame reminiscing about our elementary, junior high, and high school days. Like "Glory Days," the popular Bruce Springsteen song, we talked about the old times, our glory days, and all the fun we had growing up in Merrick on Long Island.

Then our conversation moved on to our current lives, our marriages, our children, and fatherhood. Sometime later, I told Seth about my midlife crisis and how I had turned my life around thanks to yoga, meditation, and becoming a vegetarian trending toward vegan. Even though we were sitting in the front row with a great view of the ballfield, we barely paid attention to the game. We were too immersed in catching up. I recall being so focused on my conversation with Seth that when I looked at the scoreboard, it was the 6th inning, and I did not recall how any runs had been scored that night.

After the game, I drove Seth back to his hotel. We agreed it was great seeing each other after all these years and promised to do this again before the passage of another decade. At home at the end of a wonderful evening, I wondered if my spirit guides knew who was going to unexpectedly visit me next. I didn't have to wait too long to find out.

This time, out of the blue, I was contacted by Jeff Yonteff, an old friend of mine from my summer days at Camp Schodack in Nassau, NY, in the foothills of the Berkshires near Albany. Jeff told me that he decided to take his son, Alex, on a father-son adventure during the summer and, of all places they could have chosen to go, they picked Kansas City. There, Jeff said, he and Alex would get to visit the National Collegiate Basketball Hall of Fame, tour Arrowhead Stadium, and see the Royals play a night game at the K. Jeff told me that growing up as a Yankee fan, he had always admired seeing the beautiful fountains at Kauffman Stadium on television and was anxious to see them in person. I don't know if Jeff had manifested his vision to one day visit the fountains at the K, but he did tell me that this was something he had been looking forward to for most of his life.

During the time Jeff and Alex were in KC, I arranged to meet them with Nate at the National College Basketball Hall of Fame and we spent a very enjoyable afternoon together walking around the museum and shooting hoops. Jeff and I took this opportunity to share some old camp stories and provide updates on other camp friends we were still in touch with. I found out from Jeff, after the Yonteff boys returned home, that they did get to see a Royals game at the K, and Jeff was able to cross something off of his bucket list, seeing the famous water fountains at Kauffman Stadium in person.

Just as my spirit guides and *guardian* angels had predicted, I received random visits from Seth Kornbluth, an old friend from my childhood, and from Jeff Yonteff, an old friend from summer camp. I wondered if that was it, or would another surprise visitor come to my home town. My spirit guides did not disappoint. Shortly thereafter, Derek Bauer, another friend from my past, an older fraternity brother from my college years at Tulane, contacted me to say he would be coming to Kansas City. However, I must admit, by this time I wasn't quite as surprised as I was when I learned that Seth and then Jeff told me they were coming.

In Derek's case, he was visiting Kansas City to attend a law conference. He reached out to me on Facebook, invited me to dinner and a Royals game, and we finalized our arrangements for his visit. As previously planned, I picked Derek up at his downtown hotel and we drove straight to Kauffman Stadium. We entered the K as the sun was setting, grabbed a couple of beers and reminisced about the good old fraternity days in college at Tulane. We stood with our sunglasses on, staring right into the sunset with the famous Kauffman Stadium fountains just beneath us. I joked that it felt like we were hanging out in baseball heaven.

Catching up with Derek, I marveled at how some friendships can extend years without contact, yet once renewed, feel as if no time has passed. It occurred to me that Derek, Seth and Jeff might be soul mates of mine who came to Kansas City to check in on me, to make sure that I was alright and doing well. It also occurred to me that perhaps the Baseball Gods played a role in arranging their visits since so much of the time we spent together revolved around baseball, the Royals, and Kauffman Stadium.

Derek and I found our seats just as the Royals trotted out of the dugout to their positions on the field. Out came the Royals starting pitcher, Ian Kennedy, who happens to be my neighbor down the street in Leawood. I mentioned to Derek that I had chatted with Kennedy a few times while walking my dogs, Charlie and Buddy. During one dog walk with Nate by my side, Nate got to meet Kennedy and told him that he was one of his favorite players. On another dog walk with Nate, Kennedy showed him how to throw his Vulcan Change-up. Nate was one happy kid that day.

After the second inning, I mentioned to Derek that Nate's baseball team had a tournament game that night that had just been scheduled the day before. Since I had never missed one of Nate's ballgames, I asked Derek if he would be willing to leave the Royals game a little early so we could watch Nate play. Derek was happy to comply.

Later, when we left the K and headed west on highway I-435, darkness had fallen across the beautiful Kansas City skyline. As we pulled off the highway and started driving down a dark road, Derek turned to me and said jokingly that this was exactly the kind of road he feared. No doubt he remembered what he and the older fraternity brothers had put me through when I was pledging our fraternity at Tulane. Derek asked me at that moment if I planned to drop him off in the middle of nowhere to get my revenge for all the pranks I was forced to endure as pledge back then. Since I remember my fun-filled fraternity days at Tulane fondly, even the hazing that the older brothers put me through, I told Derek that all was forgiven. We spent the next few minutes rehashing the night neither one of us will ever forget, the night known as "The Cemetery Run."

By way of background, Derek was a super friendly guy during Rush Week at the fraternity house near the Tulane campus. He reminded me of the character Eric Stratton, the proud rush chairman of his fraternity in the classic comedy

Animal House. In the movie, Stratton would self-importantly walk around the frat party, shaking hands saying, "Eric Stratton, damn glad to meet you!" In fact, the members of my pledge class all agreed that Derek was one of the nicest fraternity brothers we had met during that week. However, as soon as we were officially accepted as pledges, Derek took on a much different persona.

Once pledging began, Derek emerged as a strict taskmaster with the alter ego name of "Mr. D," and I quickly learned that he had a "dark" side. Frequently, he would bark orders at me and my pledge brothers in the fraternity house, and when he asked us to do things for him, he required that we call him "Mr. D." Mr. D demanded our attention and respect, and I believe every one of us feared him.

One night after cleaning up from dinner at the frat house, Mr. D came over to chat with me and Andy Spector, my fellow pledge brother. He said that he and another brother were going out for drinks and asked if we wanted to join them. Mr. D said that it would be a low-key evening, just to hang out, not pledge brother stuff. Andy and I looked at each other with a sense of relief and agreed to join them.

Our first stop was The Boot, a popular bar near Tulane's campus, where we all casually enjoyed a few beers and played some pool. After our billiards game, Mr. D suggested we extend the evening and go barhopping. I recall at the time, being only a lowly pledge, feeling honored to have been asked to join these older brothers for the evening.

By the time we hit the fourth bar on our night out, Andy and I were relaxed, the drinks had kicked in, and we were having a blast. For a moment, we almost forgot that we were both just pledges. Mr. D was so much fun to hang out with that night. As a matter of fact, we felt like we were out with the "old Derek" that we knew from Rush Week, not the fraternity house militant Mr. D that we feared.

After we left the fourth bar, we started driving into a part of New Orleans that I had never seen before. The streets were dark and the homes were run-down. It was way past midnight at this point, and there were no other cars on the narrow, bumpy roads we were traveling on. As we slowly drove right next to a century-old cemetery, it occurred to me that we were no longer near Tulane or its neighboring bar scene. That's when the car stopped and the engine was turned off. The happy vibration I was feeling just a few minutes ago was now gone. The silence was creepy, and without a lamppost in sight, the darkness and the evening fog made the situation seem eerier. Then we realized that jovial Rush Week, beer drinking, billiard playing Derek was gone, and angry, militant, fraternity house Mr. D had returned. Mr. D turned around in the passenger seat, and in a slow but stern voice, with a sinister look on his face, explained what was about to take place.

Mr. D said that to our left was a cemetery. Actually, it was an above-ground cemetery common to New Orleans due to its high-water level. He told us to immediately get out of the car and find a way to get to the other side of the cemetery on foot before they did by car. If they drove around and got to the other side of the cemetery before we did, they were leaving and not coming back. I wasn't sure if these guys were pranking us or not. I started to think about the story my dad told me about, when he pledged his college fraternity decades ago. My dad and one of his pledge brothers were dropped off in the middle of the night in the middle of nowhere somewhere on Long Island on the last night of pledging known as Hell Night. They were told that if they didn't find a way back to their fraternity house in the Bronx by sunrise, they would be black-balled. Just as I finished thinking about my dad's fraternity experience, I heard Mr. D scream "Get out of the car—now!"

The real irony of this predicament was that just a few weeks prior, I was speaking with my parents on the phone and had actually bragged that my fraternity pledge experience had been so much fun so far. I recall boasting that pledging was actually too easy, and not what I expected. I literally joked that the fraternity brothers really should be hazing us harder. Well, the lesson here is be careful what you think and what you say out loud because the universe is always listening. Perhaps our thoughts and words have the power to manifest into reality, both in positive and, in this case, negative ways as well.

Drunk and honestly terrified, we sprinted across that cemetery like escaped convicts running away from prison with hungry guard dogs on our trail. With no time to think, we were weaving through the cemetery headstones, where the dead were respectfully buried and laid to rest, like downhill slalom skiers curving around gates on an Olympic qualifying trial run. I felt like I was running for my life. At the same time, I kept an eye on Andy, who seemed as scared as I was, to make sure we both made it safely to the other side of the cemetery.

We did reach the other side of the cemetery together, but there was no easy exit in sight, only a fence topped with barbed wire. We had no choice but to try to hop it. However, with the ground wet and soggy from a recent rain, my sneakers kept slipping as I tried to climb the fence. I simply could not gain enough traction. Each time I tried, I would slide back down.

After my last failed attempt to hop the fence, I could see car lights in the distance growing brighter through the fog and I knew my time was up. With one last chance to make it over the fence, I climbed on top of a headstone and hoisted myself up using my foot to push off of it. Pushing with all my might, I was able to grab the top of the fence with both hands, but as I pulled to hoist myself up and over, my left hand got punctured by a sharp, tiny blade. Now, my left hand and I were stuck on the barbed wire. I was in serious pain, but the adrenalin rushing through my body must have been more powerful. With no more time to be afraid and little time to think, I ripped my hand out of the barbed wire and jumped for my life.

Just as I landed on the ground on the other side of the fence, the car pulled up. As Andy and I got into the car, we realized that my left hand was gushing blood. Mr. D, initially excited to congratulate us on our achievement, saw my facial expression, then my hand, and then the blood, and now he was the one who was scared. Clearly, Mr. D knew that his pledge prank had gone terribly wrong.

We drove to the Tulane Medical Center and as I was being treated in the Emergency Room for my badly cut and bleeding hand, I said to Mr. D, "You better make sure that I am untouchable from now on. I have paid my dues." Mr. D said, "I promise," and he kept his word. I was untouchable for the rest of the semester.

By the way, my dad did make it back from Long Island to his fraternity house in the Bronx on his Hell Night. More than five decades later, two of his life-long best friends are his fraternity brothers, and he still sees a dozen or so of his brothers every year in Delray Beach, Florida at mini reunions. Both my dad and I seem to have taken full advantage of what fraternity life is all about.

As Derek and I continued our drive from Kauffman Stadium to Nate's tournament baseball game, we agreed that the cemetery run prank was one for the record books. We arrived at Nate's game in progress, just as he was coming up to the plate for his at bat. Derek got to see Nate earn a walk, steal second base, and then third. I turned to Derek and said, "Watch, Nate will score on a wild pitch." The next pitch was a fastball in the dirt that went through the catcher's legs. Nate jumped at the chance and ran for home, scoring the first run of the game. As he had done many times before, Nate had turned a walk into a home run.

That night, after driving Derek back to his hotel in the city, I gave my cemetery run adventure a little more thought. I certainly enjoyed retelling that story with Derek a thousand times more than I did experiencing it years ago. Thinking about it also reminded me of the Bruce Springsteen song, "We Are Alive," in which he describes a graveyard where the deceased lie alone, buried in the dark. However, in the lyrics Springsteen expresses his view of the difference between the bodies buried left to rot and the souls and spirits that rise above their graves and ascend into the afterlife. In this song, the listener hears the voices of the dead crying out, telling their life stories and explaining how they died. The souls sing the chorus: "We are alive. And though our bodies lie alone here in the dark, our spirits rise to carry the fire and light the spark. To stand shoulder to shoulder and heart to heart." Springsteen eases our concern with his words, "Let your mind rest easy, sleep well my friend, it's only our bodies that betray us in the end." His message, while bodies may die, their souls live on.

I have come to accept the possibility that some souls return to earth after death for another chance at life, while other more accomplished souls remain in another dimension that some call heaven. Some may become spirit guides and *guardian* angels to their loved ones still alive here on earth and some may be looking out for us from the other side of the veil, like the Baseball Gods. The best depiction of these angelic beings of light, in relation to baseball, is shown in the films *Angels in the Outfield* and its sequel, *Angels in the Infield*.

CHAPTER TWELVE

Angels in the Infield

"Angels speak to those who silence their minds long enough to hear."
—Proverb

AN ANGEL IS GENERALLY DEPICTED IN RELIGIOUS TEXTS as a supernatural being. Interestingly, they are similarly described in various world religions and mythologies, often portrayed as loving and kind celestial beings who act as representatives of God and function as intermediaries between humans, God, heaven and earth. It is believed by many that angels carry out God's requests to guide and protect human beings here on earth. Whenever I see actors portrayed as angels on television or in movies, they are usually shown with wings on their backs, halos on their heads, often surrounded by a bright white light. Paintings of angels on display in the religion section of the finest museums around the world follow this description. In baseball terms, my favorite depiction of angels can be seen in the movie *Angels in the Outfield* and, in its sequel, *Angels in the Infield*.

Angels in the Infield, directed by Robert King, begins with an angel sitting on a bench in heaven waiting for his chance to get into a ballgame. The scene reminded me of the times I sat on the bench as a sophomore of my high school varsity soccer team waiting for my opportunity to play. The angel asks for one more chance to go back down to earth. As I watched this opening scene, my first reaction was that the angel's request was a reference to reincarnation.

In the next scene, Eddie Everett, the main character in the movie portrayed by actor Patrick Warburton (who also played the role of David Puddy, Elaine Benes' boyfriend, in the classic comedy sitcom *Seinfeld*), gets a cell phone call while standing for the national anthem before the game is about to start. Yes, Eddie, the starting pitcher, is so arrogant that he has no qualms about having his mobile phone with him on the baseball field. His level of disrespect increases as he holds his cell phone to his ear during the national anthem to approve stock trades. "Buy 80 shares of Microsoft and sell Merck," Eddie says.

Later in the film in a flashback, we learn that Eddie was once a star rookie pitching sensation who had made it to the show with the Anaheim Angels. Eddie's baseball career was off to a great start and thanks to his outstanding pitching, his team made it deep into the postseason playing in the American League Championship Series. They were just one out away from making it to the World Series. Unfortunately, as fate would have it, Eddie chokes and makes an error on a ground ball that costs his team the game and the series. Eddie's pitching career and his life are never the same after that play. His baseball career takes a tumble, his wife divorces him, and a deep depression settles in.

In the movie, we learn that Eddie is also the father of an adorable young girl that he never made time for. When Eddie's ex-wife decides to relocate from LA to Boston for a new job, his daughter has no choice but to move in with him. When she does, she sees how unhappy, shallow and unfulfilling her Dad's life is. Frankly, she sees he's a mess. Eddie is still haunted by the error he made during that big playoff game when he was a rookie. He cannot seem to forgive himself for his miscue and cannot move on with his life.

As you might expect in a movie like this, Eddie's daughter decides to ask God to help her father find his way back. She prays for Eddie to get another chance to be the baseball player he could have been. Deep down I sensed that she was also praying for her dad to become a better, more attentive, more caring father as well. Hearing her prayers, an angel is sent down to earth from the heavens to help her help her father.

Although advertised as a comedy and a fantasy, *Angels in the Infield* deals with a few serious, thought-provoking themes. One such theme is that angels may be real, but they respect the free will bestowed upon mankind. They are here to help but cannot do so unless asked. The way they are asked is through prayer. For prayer to work, there must be faith.

It is during another critical game late in the season that Eddie begins his spiritual awakening, with the help of an angel and his daughter. Eddie's daughter is in the dugout with the team when she sees an angel standing next to one of the players. She excitedly tells Eddie that she knows that this player has faith in God and is certain to get a hit. Eddie, trusting his daughter, convinces the team manager to put in a pinch hitter at a crucial spot during the game. Not only that, but Eddie suggests that the manager put in the worst hitter on the team. When the coach reluctantly agrees, the movie's special effects show the angel's essence shift into the player body. The pinch hitter, the least likely player on the team, now possessing the power and energy of the Holy Spirit, sure enough, gets a base hit. In a typical movie fashion, Eddie goes from a washed-up has-been to a hero.

While *Angels in the Infield* delivers some life lessons and deep spiritual messages, it's still primarily a comedy. Perhaps the funniest scene in the movie occurs when Eddie, on the mound talking to his catcher, can't get a certain tune out of his head. Eddie hums it. His catcher recognizes the tune and replies that it's Beethoven's Ninth in B minor, known as Ode to Joy. This leads to a very funny conversation as the players gather around the pitcher's mound and debate the name of this famous piece of classical music.

This humorous moment in *Angels in the Infield* cleverly pays homage to a classic scene in the film *Bull Durham*, where the players gather around the pitcher's mound for a similar type of conversation. Here, rookie pitcher Ebby Calvin "Nuke" LaLoosh, played by actor Tim Robbins, suddenly can't seem to throw strikes. All of his pitchers are wild and outside. In the dugout, the manager and the coaches are talking about what may be wrong with LaLoosh. Finally, catcher "Crash" Davis, the main character in the film played by Kevin Costner, calls a time out, approaches LaLoosh on the mound, and asks, "What's wrong?" LaLoosh replies, "I'm a little nervous, my old man is here." Sure enough, Crash looks over and sees LaLoosh's dad in the stands right behind home plate in the front row with a huge over-the-shoulder camera taking videos.

Then the infield players join them and gather at the pitcher's mound. The first player mentions that another player on the team just got engaged and he needs an engagement gift. Then, the second baseman Jose shows up very upset and talking to himself in Spanish. He says, "Hey you guys, don't throw me anything. My girlfriend put a curse on my glove." LaLoosh says confidently, "I'll take the hex off the f*&%king glove, give me the glove." Since Jose believes in superstitious rituals, he says, "Well then, you've got to cut the head off a live rooster." Finally, the frustrated team manager tells the bench coach to get out there and see what's going on.

The bench coach arrives at the pitcher's mound with his hands inside his pockets and says, "What the hell is going on here?" Crash breaks it down for the coach. "Well, Nuke's scared because his eyelids are jammed and his old man is here. We need a…was it a live rooster? (looking at Jose to confirm) …We need a live rooster to take the curse off Jose's glove, and nobody seems to know what to get Millie and Jimmy for their wedding present." Crash looks around the group of players to confirm, "Is that about right?" Spoken like a team leader protecting his players, Crash says, "We're dealing with a lot of shit." The bench coach takes it all in while chewing a giant wad of gum and thoughtfully replies, "Well, candle sticks always make a nice gift and maybe find out where she is registered and get her maybe a place setting, or maybe a silverware pattern is good. Ok, let's get to it!" He claps his hands and breaks up the meeting on the mound.

As a devoted baseball fan and movie lover, I still laugh out loud whenever I see this famous scene in *Bull Durham*. I even laughed as I was writing about it for this book. And now, thanks to that movie, every time I see a meeting on the mound at a baseball game, I wonder if the players are talking about the tense situation occurring on the ballfield or simply joking with each other and taking a short break from the game.

Like *Bull Durham*, the storyline in *Angels in the Infield* intertwines serious topics and life lessons around humor. By the end of the movie, Eddie overcomes his midlife crisis, and moves forward with his life to become a better person. In a true Hollywood happy ending, he also restores his relationship with his daughter. With the help of an angel, her prayers are answered.

As a spiritual person who does yoga and meditates on a daily basis, one of my lasting memories from *Angels in the Infield* occurs when an angel cavalierly gives advice to a little girl and says, "Deep thought and meditation always work!" I would agree.

CHAPTER THIRTEEN

The Baseball Player's Guide to Meditation

"I feel like I'm in a bubble of serenity, going through my deliveries one at a time. All around me is craziness, even 60-feet away there's something I could be fearful about–but I'm staying in that bubble of solitude and calm, which comes from my practice of Transcendental Meditation."

—Barry Zito

THE ANCIENT YOGIS BELIEVED THAT WHEN THEY meditated, angels swirled around them and beckon to help. When people pray, they ask for help. Therein lies the subtle difference between meditation and prayer. When people pray, they are communicating to the universe. When people meditate, they allow the universe to speak to them.

While it may be difficult at times to measure its spiritual benefits, there is convincing evidence that the daily practice of meditation has measurable health benefits. Meditation has been proven to improve the body's immunity system, reduce emotional stress, reduce inflammation, reduce pain, and even lower a person's blood pressure and cholesterol levels. Modern science has supported these findings using sophisticated tools like neuroimaging, functional magnetic resonance imaging, brain mapping technology and gene research, allowing scientists and researchers greater knowledge and insight than previously available.

I have personally experienced some of these health benefits. After adding a daily yoga and meditation practice to my life and changing my eating habits more than two years ago, my blood pressure and cholesterol levels decreased, and I have lost a significant amount of weight. I have also seen an improvement in my immune system's ability to protect me. For example, every year the flu season seems to get worse than the year before. Yet in the last ten years, thankfully, I have not gotten the flu, even with foregoing the flu shot during this period. Also, I have seen a decrease in the pain I experience in my fingers and hands from arthritis. Perhaps I have angels swirling around me.

While it seems clear that yoga, meditation and eating better may be keeping me healthier, these relaxing, thought-provoking activities may also be enhancing my ability as a financial advisor as I run Satya, my asset management firm. I can see this in my investment performance results. Since starting my daily yoga and meditation routine, I also found the time and energy to become an author. In addition to writing books about baseball, of which this is the second with number three currently in draft, I plan to pen a series of books about music and investing, two additional subjects I am also passionate about.

It is also reasonable to assume that meditation has played a role in improving athletic performance on the baseball field. My research revealed that some baseball teams have been using this technique as a strategic weapon since the 1970s, and many continue to do so to this day.

The Philadelphia Phillies were one of the first teams to embrace the potential benefits of meditation. The Phillies began the early 1970s as cellar dwellers at the bottom of their division in the National League. Interestingly, after implementing a meditation routine, they emerged as division winners later in the decade. In the mid-1980s, some players on the Oakland A's embraced the practice of meditation and the team also had a mental skills coach on their staff in 1989, the year they won the World Series. As highlighted in the previous chapter on veganism, the Chicago Cubs embraced meditation in their organization after manager Joe Maddon arrived on the scene. Amazingly, shortly thereafter, the team broke their 108-year curse and won the World Series in 2016.

Individually, several baseball players have spoken publicly about their meditation practice. The great ex-New York Yankee short stop Derek Jeter said in an interview in 2012 that he did one-hour morning meditations as part of his off-day routine. One wonders if this helped the Yankees win five World Series championships while Jeter was there. Pitcher Barry Zito has been a long-time advocate of meditation and he won two World Series rings and an American League Cy Young Award. During a sad time in baseball history when many players were cheating by using steroids to hit home runs, Shawn Green, who hit 328 home runs in his career during the 1990s, became a power hitter using meditation as his secret weapon. This is confirmed in his book, *The Way of Baseball: Finding Stillness at 95 MPH*, in which Green credits much of his success in baseball to his meditation practice. Shawn Green not only meditates, he also does yoga.

CHAPTER FOURTEEN

The Yogis in the Outfield

"Rule the mind or it will rule you."
—Buddha

IN AUGUST 2017 KATIE BAKER WROTE AN ARTICLE, "A Freak Accident: Michael Conforto's Injury Sums Up the Mets' Lost Season," in which she describes a rarely-seen injury that occurred when Conforto swung his bat in the bottom of the 5th inning in a game against the Arizona Diamondbacks. With a routine swing of his bat, Conforto dislocated his shoulder ending his season. Perhaps more interesting, Conforto's freak mishap was the 26th injury of the season for the New York Mets. Since I am convinced that athletes who practice yoga incur fewer injuries, I wondered if the Mets embraced yoga as a part of their fitness program.

While researching whether the Mets instruct their players to practice yoga, I learned that many ballplayers, both at the professional and college level, have embraced yoga over the last few years. Jon Perrin told me that when he injured his pitching arm in college, yoga was introduced as an important part of his rehab process. In fact, Perrin said that yoga was one of the first activities he was cleared to do. Working his body back into shape, Perrin did yoga four times a week before he was permitted to pick up any hand weights heavier than five pounds.

The baseball season is long and grueling, stretching over 162 games. It is even longer and more intense for the teams that make the playoffs. As the season grinds on, year after year, a baseball player's body tends to slowly break down. A daily yoga routine will help players avoid injuries, or lessen their severity, because the stretching and body movements performed doing yoga will increase muscle flexibility and reduce the chance of straining or pulling muscles. In addition to preventing or reducing the extent of injuries, yoga can help athletes improve their explosiveness, speed and balance, and will increase their strength.

While the benefits of a daily yoga routine during the season are clear, it may be ever more beneficial for ballplayers to do yoga in the offseason. Baseball requires players to perform many repetitive motions. As a result, they, like golfers and tennis players, are more likely to injury themselves due to the overuse of certain muscles. Overuse injuries include muscle strains, stress fractures, bone dislocations, ligament tears, tendonitis and bursitis. My research on this subject revealed, convincingly, that yoga was effective in reducing injury rates and the time required to recover from those injuries. It follows that adding a yoga practice in the offseason will extend its benefits into the next baseball season when it arrives.

In my opinion, yoga may be the next strategic weapon for baseball management to employ on a broad basis. In the same way that many savvy front offices now embrace the study of a new breed of in-depth statistics, known as sabermetrics, to gain an advantage over their competition, early implementers of yoga will be one step ahead of the pack.

For proof of my "baseball yoga thesis," let's take another look at the Milwaukee Brewers.

The Brewers included yoga as part of their spring training exercise sessions in 2017. A year later, in 2018, they found themselves one game away from playing in the World Series. The Brewers' extended their yoga program to their minor league affiliates as well. Perrin told me that the Brewers did yoga frequently during spring training and the yoga sessions continued while he played for the Colorado Springs Sky Sox.

Individually, several baseball players outside of the Brewers organization have embraced yoga, including Giancarlo Stanton, who won the 2017 National League MVP award playing with the Miami Marlins. Now a New York Yankees outfielder, Stanton has so enthusiastically embraced yoga that he teamed up with Gaiam, a yoga company, to make a *Yoga for Power* instructional video for athletes. Watching Stanton perform his yoga poses will quickly dispel any myths that yoga is just for soccer moms wearing the latest style of Lululemon pants. Other power-hitting baseball players that do yoga include Jim Thome, a recent Hall of Fame inductee, and Alex Rodriguez, the retired Seattle Mariner shortstop and thereafter, the New York Yankee third baseman.

As more and more ballplayers embraced yoga, it was inevitable that baseball fans across the country would follow suit. From Dodger Stadium in Los Angeles to Nationals Park in Washington, DC, hosting a yoga day at the ballpark has become an annual tradition. The Kansas City Royals have hosted a *Yoga Day at the K* for the past several seasons. The yoga trend is evident in the minor leagues as well. For example, in 2015, the Triple-A Iowa Cubs in Des Moines, hosted a yoga day at their ballpark and had about 400 participants at their inaugural event. Iowa Cubs players joined their fans and they did yoga on the field together.

With the benefits of yoga and meditation becoming more widespread, and therefore more popular in baseball and elsewhere, the Baseball Gods must be pleased. It should be noted that yoga and meditation are not required by the Baseball Gods, but they do have some rules that must be adhered to. That's why I entitled the next chapter *The Rules of the Baseball Gods*.

CHAPTER FIFTEEN

The Rules of the Baseball Gods

"Baseball gives...a growing boy self-poise and self-reliance.
Baseball is a man maker."
—Al Spalding

AS I BECAME DISILLUSIONED WITH ORGANIZED RELIGION
during my teen years, I thought that the stories in the Bible,
in the Torah and in other religious texts were conceived by
a bunch of old wise men contemplating ways to control the
behavior of the masses in a what seemed to be a lawless society. This view of religion stayed with me for the next 30 years
of my life. Then I experienced a mid-life crisis and I knew that
to escape it, I had to find a new direction.

By the time my daughter Kayla became a Bat Mitzvah, I
was already well-travelled on the spiritual path I had chosen.
I became a yogi and I found inner peace, happiness and optimism. During this transformative period, I became familiar
with Eastern religions, such as Hinduism and Buddhism, and
spent time exploring new age concepts, such as channeling
and astrology. After absorbing my fill of new age literature, I
discovered books dealing with Jewish concepts that previously
I knew little about, such as Gilgul, Musar and Kabbalah.

Sitting in the front row at synagogue for Kayla's Bat Mitzvah, proudly watching my no-longer little girl chant from the Torah, I questioned for the first time in my life whether these old wise men created all of these stories themselves. Alternatively, I wondered if they received guidance from angels, from another energy source, or even directly from God. I opened my mind to the possibility that these biblical allegories and legendary tales were in fact channeled to these wise men from such a source.

I envisioned these wise men sitting in caves or on hilltops surrounded by candlelight or a burning fire chanting, meditating and deep in prayer. As they reached a complete meditative state, the automatic, robotic writing would begin. I visualized the wise men intently writing down every word that was telepathically being sent to them from another dimension. After decades of doubt, I could now see how the Torah and the *Book of John* might have indeed been written by men who were channeling the Holy Spirit as they wrote the divine word. I could also now see these stories from a gnostic perspective. These religious words could be taken literally, or they could be taken as a very sophisticated series of metaphors with hidden occult knowledge.

Taking this channeling concept a step further, I wondered if I may have been similarly influenced as an author. When drafting my first book, with almost 60,000 words in it, I recall putting on my headphones during the writing process and jamming out to live concerts on my nugs.net app on my iPhone. After a few minutes of listening to the music, I would get into my own meditative state, so to speak. As I got into the rhythm, I got immersed in my writing. Words and ideas started cascading out of me like never before and just kept coming. Soon after, I opened my mind to the real possibility that I could be channeling my creative writing ideas from another dimension.

Sometimes ideas for my books come to me during yoga or meditation, or when I exercise. One beautiful, cool, sunny, Kansas City morning, I decided to go out for a jog. I started with a fast walk, as I usually do, worked it up to a slow jog and then increased my speed to the pace I wanted to maintain. After 15 minutes or so, thoughts for this book started to flood into my mind. It was during this jog that I got the idea for *"The Rules of the Baseball Gods."* Once the initial concept came to me, rules started to flow one after the other. Every few minutes, I stopped jogging to write them down in my phone, and here they are.

The Rules of The Baseball Gods:

1. No ball playing in the house.
2. No talking about a no-hitter during a no-hitter.
3. Never try to hit a home run. If you try, you will ground out, pop out, or worse, strike out.
4. Never give up, never give in.
5. Respect your umpires, coaches, teammates, the other team, your parents, your siblings, the game of baseball, and most importantly, yourself.
6. No negative thinking. If you think you will make an error, you probably will.
7. No sore losers. Learning how to win is not as important as learning how to lose.

8. If it ain't broke, don't fix it.
9. No excuses. Take credit for a good play but also responsibility for a bad play.
10. Play to have fun and for the love of the game.

I drafted these rules as if they were the Ten Commandments. Good karma is created by obeying them and bad karma is created when they are broken.

Of course, there are many other rules in baseball, many unwritten, that should also be obeyed. These unwritten rules are learned by baseball players slowly over time, mastered from years of experience, and have been passed down from generation to generation by coaches and players. "The Unwritten Rules of Baseball" differ from the basic rudimentary rules of baseball, such as three strikes and you're out, four balls and you walk, and games are nine innings long. The unwritten rules also differ from "*The Rules of the Baseball Gods*" in that they focus on etiquette, sportsmanship, conventional wisdom and accepted codes of conduct. By including some of these unwritten rules of baseball in this book, I am doing my part to pass this sacred knowledge on to others.

Former baseball player, author and television analyst Doug Glanville wrote about this topic in "Baseball's Unwritten Rules," an op-ed piece published in the *New York Times*. Glanville wrote, "Who does it really hurt when you celebrate a home run a little more enthusiastically than your opponents feel is appropriate, or when I steal second with my team already up by 7, or vehemently argue a call in the ninth inning of a game we're winning by 13 runs. Who really cares?" Glanville answers his own questions by saying "Sportsmanship cares, for starters. After a Little League game, the players shake hands. We play by the rules, we honor our history, we respect our opponent. Sportsmanship is not quantifiable; we say we know it when we see it." Glanville rightly points out in his article that the unwritten rules of baseball help maintain good sportsmanship and integrity in the game.

Should a ballplayer disrespect the unwritten rules of baseball, there will be consequences. Typically, the rules are enforced by the manager, the coaches, the umpires, fellow players or the Baseball Gods themselves. Respecting the unwritten rules of baseball is not just appropriate behavior, it's good karma. That said, here are The Unwritten Rules of Baseball as I see them.

The Unwritten Rules of Baseball:

1. Don't step out of the batter's box once a pitcher begins his windup.
2. Don't walk in front of the catcher on the way into the batter's box.
3. Don't step in the batter's box while the pitcher is warming up.
4. Don't run into a catcher who doesn't yet possess the baseball and a catcher should not stand in the baseline before the ball arrives.
5. Don't slide into second base to take out the legs of an infielder.
6. Don't linger in the batter's box, don't flip the bat, and don't slow jog around the bases after hitting a home run.
7. Don't play aggressively with a big lead late in the game.

8. Don't step on the pitcher's mound if you're not pitching.
9. Don't talk to a pitcher in the dugout while he is throwing a no-hitter.
10. Don't bunt to break up a no-hitter.
11. Paint the corners on a 0-2 count.
12. An infielder should catch the infield fly, not the pitcher.
13. Let the center fielder get the ball.
14. What goes on in the clubhouse stays in the clubhouse.
15. Opposing players are barred from the team locker room.
16. Cheating is part of the game, but do so at your own risk.
17. Retaliate as needed.
18. Everyone joins in on the fight to stand up for your teammates.
19. The veterans sit in the front on the team bus.
20. The veterans have veto power over the music in the weight room.
21. Rookies need to pay their dues (but no excessive hazing).

Bad karma creates a debt that eventually has to be paid off. Therefore, the sooner youngsters learn the unwritten rules of baseball, the better. For most kids, this learning process starts with a father-son catch, as mine did with my dad and as Nate's did with me. It continues in Little League. For kids who don't have dads with time to spare or Little League, it continues by playing ball with friends and neighbors at nearby makeshift baseball fields scattered across our cities and suburbs, known as *the Sandlot.*

CHAPTER SIXTEEN

The Sandlot

"You're killing me, Smalls."
—Ham Porter, *The Sandlot*

THE SANDLOT, AN AMERICAN COMING-OF-AGE BASEBALL
film co-written, directed, and narrated by David Mickey
Evans, has become a cult classic. The movie tells the story of a
group of young neighborhood kids in Los Angeles who love to
play baseball during the summer of 1962, a time in American
history when life seemed more innocent and simpler. Kids
were able to roam the streets freely and safely, and after playing outdoors all day long, they came home for dinner at sunset
exhausted, dirty and hungry. I suspect the movie depicts
a childhood similar to my dad's, except he grew up in the
concrete jungle of the Bronx, not in beautiful, sunny Southern
California as did the kids in *The Sandlot*.

I am and always have been a movie lover. I got even more
interested in behind-the-scenes movie making after Reggie's
brother, Richard Devinki, moved to LA and got involved
in the business. For me, movies about baseball have special

status. Some made me laugh, as did *Bull Durham* and Major League, some affected me deeply and made me tear up, as did *Field of Dreams*, and some made me think, as did *The Natural* and *Angels in the Infield*.

Surprisingly, until recently I had not seen *The Sandlot*, even though over the years I frequently heard people make references to it in jokes. Some folks even quote from the film, as is often the case with other classic movies, like The Godfather, Swingers and The Big Lebowski. Perhaps these references to *The Sandlot* kept coming up everywhere I went because the Baseball Gods were trying to get me to see the movie.

The Sandlot celebrated the 25th anniversary of its release in 2018. In recognition, some of the players on the Milwaukee Brewers made a video during spring training recreating a famous scene in the film. The video was very funny and went viral in the baseball community. Eric Sogard, an infielder now with the Tampa Bay Rays, portrayed "Squints" with the glasses, "Ham" Porter was played by Stephen Vogt, now with the San Francisco Giants, and "Smalls" was played by outfielder Brett Phillips, now with my Kansas City Royals. After finally watching the hilarious video, two things came to mind. First, I decided that I must see this movie. Second, participating in a parody of *The Sandlot* may get you traded or released.

Thinking back now, I figured out why it took me so long to see *The Sandlot*. The film was released in 1993 when I was a freshman at Tulane. I was recently accepted as a brother in my fraternity and busy making new friends. Also, I was living in New Orleans, probably the most entertaining city in the United States. Between studying for my courses, actively participating in fraternity sports, parties, and events, and exploring Bourbon Street and its neighboring music joints, watching funk, blues and jazz bands like the Meters, Galactic and the Neville Brothers, I was simply too busy back then to take the time to watch the movie.

So, 25 years after its release, I finally saw *The Sandlot*. I loved the movie and could easily see why it had become so popular. In the film, the neighborhood kids get together to play baseball all day long. However, there are only nine of them, not enough to field two teams and complete a full game, so they are always looking for more kids to join them. When they do play, they do so for the sheer pleasure it brings them. They don't pick teams. They just take turns hitting without an official batting order and they rotate playing at each position on the field. There is a charming innocence to their approach to the game. They play because they love it. No scoreboard. No custom designed uniforms. No winning. No losing. No $400 aluminum bats. No overbearing parents yelling at the umpire for bad calls, or worse, yelling at their own kids because he or she made an error or struck out. In the beginning of the movie, Smalls had just moved to southern California after his school year ended. He was the new kid in town who knew very little about baseball. Ultimately, he fits right in with his new friends and into this baseball utopia known as *The Sandlot*.

Watching the film, I was reminded of the stories my dad used to tell me about his life as a kid, playing punchball, stickball, stoopball and other games in the city streets and schoolyards in the Bronx. Sometimes he played ball with his dad, my Grandpa Norman, and his older brother, my Uncle Eddie. They both gave him pointers to help him get better. My dad's childhood revolved around sports, from basketball and touch football on the concrete in the schoolyard and slapball on the asphalt inner city streets. My dad was always playing ball, beginning before the first school bell rang until the sun went down. No video games like Fortnite or MLB The Show 19 to play back then, just the stoop, the schoolyard and *the sandlot*.

When my dad was a kid in the 1950s, sports played in the schoolyard were rough and tough, usually self-enforced, but innocent and pure nonetheless. No parents around, no coaches around, just the self-ruled street or schoolyard where playful teasing and "talking trash" were part of the game. If you couldn't take it, you went home. Kids in the Bronx back then played for the love of the game, just like the kids in *The Sandlot*, and every youngster grew up hoping to someday become a major league ballplayer like Willie Mays, Mickey Mantle or Duke Snyder.

Despite the number of schoolyards and sandlots that exist across the land, something has changed in youth sports in America over the last few decades. Baseball for kids, like football, soccer and other youth sports, has matured into a thriving, organized, moneymaking business, especially in and around major metropolitan cities. In fact, "for profit" youth activities have an official nickname, "pay-to-play sports." I suspect author and renowned capitalist Adam Smith would be pleased to see that there are no boundaries to his economic model. On the other hand, author and Communist Karl Marx would likely be outraged that American capitalism has no limits. Hard to believe, but America has found a way to profit from something as innocent and pure as youth baseball.

I first learned about competitive, for profit youth baseball programs after moving to Kansas City, and I had my reservations. Financial cost, significant time commitment, excessive pressure on the kids to succeed, potential burnout and possible injuries from overuse were some of my initial concerns. I preferred the less competitive recreational sports model because it was more affordable and took less time away time from what should be parents first priority for their kids— education. Admittedly, I was also reluctant to embrace the competitive baseball sports model because it was less likely that I would get to be a coach, which I did and so enjoyed when Nate and his friends played on local recreational baseball teams.

However, it became clear to me that my baseball coaching days were over when Nate turned 11. Apparently, the Baseball Gods had carefully planned a series of events that would direct him towards competitive baseball. First, Nate's local recreational baseball team disbanded because its head coach resigned after only one season. Then, picking up Nate after a sleepover at his friend's house, the friend's mother and I chatted about other baseball options that might be available to our kids. Finally, later that night in a text, she told me that the Kansas City Blaze, a local competitive baseball club, would be holding tryouts the next day looking for three new players to complete their roster.

Most competitive baseball teams hold tryouts as much as nine months before the season begins. Their rosters are typically filled for months before the first pitch of the new season is thrown. However, the Blaze had unexpectedly lost three players to another competitive team and needed to fill those open spots quickly. I knew right away that this open door came courtesy of the Baseball Gods and I accepted the invitation for Nate. The next day at the tryouts, Nate played great and was offered a roster spot on the team.

I soon learned that there are benefits to being a member of a competitive baseball team. For example, the Blaze rent an indoor practice facility for their players to use every day of the week, rain or shine, all year long. The facility is equipped with batting cages, an artificial turf infield and bullpen pitching mounds. Now, rather than playing catch with Nate on our driveway, I could drive Nate to the Blaze facility for him to practice whenever we had time to spare.

After Nate earned his spot on the Blaze roster, we took full advantage of their facility. Due to my somewhat flexible business schedule, Nate and I would often practice at odd hours and have the entire facility to ourselves. Nate took batting practice, fielded grounders and practiced his pitching on cold days during October, November and December, and on bitter cold days during the winter months of January, February and March as well. Nate practiced on rainy days too. Nate loved every minute of it, and so did I.

In addition to our father-son practices, Nate was also participating in weekly offseason practices at the Blaze indoor facility with his new teammates and coaches, even though the baseball season was still months away. These practice sessions were intense and impressive. The coaching staff ran them like a well-oiled machine, with players smoothly rotating from one drill to the next. Every practice included defensive drills and batting practice. I suspect the coaches had seen practice sessions at the college or major league level and they implemented some of the drills for the Blaze players to follow. The coaches even required the team to dress in uniform during their workouts.

It was actually exciting for me to watch the youngsters on the team seamlessly turn double plays during infield practice drills. I tried to recall if I had ever seen Nate's recreational team turn a double play at practice or in a game but couldn't. These boys were turning them as if they had been doing so for years. Before the kids could catch their breath from turning double plays, they were off to the soft toss batting area where each player got some one-on-one time with a professional coach. Then, while some players were working on their pitching techniques, others were getting swings hitting off a baseball tee. Another group of players stood at the batting cages waiting their turn for some more reps.

An indoor baseball facility and a group of excellent coaches do not come cheap. In fact, they are expensive. While Reggie and I are blessed to be able to afford the cost for Nate to join a baseball club like the Blaze, I realize that many parents do not have the resources to do so for their kids. My grandpa Norman was one of those kids. My dad was also one of those kids. At times, watching Nate and his teammates practice at the Blaze facility, I would ponder the implications of "pay-to-play" youth sports and their long-term impact on American society.

There was a time, decades ago, when top-tier baseball clubs and "travel" teams were reserved for elite athletes only. Now, competitive teams have become more commonplace in the American sports landscape. Kansas City, for example, has many competitive soccer clubs and when I googled "baseball academy and clubs in Kansas City," the results yielded a long list. The reason for this is simple. Follow the money. From sophisticated sports equipment to custom uniforms and merchandise to private lessons and coaching, youth sports have become a really big business.

As an entrepreneur who founded his own investment firm, I could appreciate and respect that these organizations have significant costs to run their operations. Overhead costs incurred by a baseball club include leasing ballfields and facilities, hiring licensed coaches, buying bats, baseballs, helmets and other equipment and paying for insurance. The capitalist in me recognized that entrepreneurs saw a void in the sports marketplace and found a profitable way to fill that space and, at the same time, meet a growing demand. Another part of me, perhaps on a more emotional level, felt sad about this development. I thought pay-to-play sports could be undermining the American dream. I was concerned that for-profit youth sports breeds exclusivity and limits cultural diversity.

My concerns were alleviated somewhat when I learned about the grand opening of the Kansas City Urban Youth Academy. During the summer of 2017 Nate attended Dayton Moore's week-long baseball camp at the JCC in Overland Park. On the last day of camp, the kids boarded school buses and traveled downtown to play baseball at the new, privately financed $19-million-dollar baseball complex, co-sponsored by Major League Baseball and the Kansas City Royals. The goal of the academy is to make available to inner city kids, at no cost, the same quality coaching and training offered by competitive clubs to level the playing field. The academy in Kansas City was the 9th facility of its kind sponsored by MLB. The kids who participate in the Kansas City Urban Youth

Academy now have terrific new baseball fields to play on and an indoor facility where they can learn about other aspects of the game, such as umpiring, ushering, grounds keeping and sports writing. As an avid baseball fan, and as a parent, I couldn't be more pleased with this development.

In Aaron Randle's article on this subject, "Cutting-edge Baseball Academy About to Open at 18th and Vine, But Who Will Come Play?" I was not surprised to learn that the Academy is a dream project of Dayton Moore, the general manager of the Royals, and the driving force behind its implementation. According to the article, the Academy will cost more than $500,000 in annual upkeep, which will be wholly financed and managed by the Royals organization for the next 20 years. Moore is a baseball executive with both a vision and a heart. Learning about this very promising countertrend in youth baseball, I felt a newfound sense that all was well in youth baseball in America.

As the winter turned to springtime, Nate's Blaze team started practicing outdoors, rather than inside the club's training facility, except on rainy days. The coaches emphasized infield and outfield defensive drills during the first few outdoor practice sessions. I guess they realize that throwing out an opposing team's player on his way to home plate is just as important as hitting a home run. On the day of the 4th outdoor practice, the coaches decided a scrimmage, a practice game, was in order. The coaches selected two team captains and then had the rest of the players line up for a draft, just the way my dad told me they used to do it in the schoolyard when he was a kid.

The Blaze roster was not designed to field two complete teams. Typically, these teams have just enough kids for one team, with a few substitutes. Therefore, for a scrimmage during practice, the coaches need a few extra players. I was sitting on a small hill behind the first base line when I noticed that no one was playing center field. I caught Coach Dean Wright's eye and knew I had read his mind when he said, "Mr. Fink, would you help us out and play center field?"

Yes, I know. I'm an adult, I'm a parent, and I'm older than many of the Nate's coaches, but for a moment I was a kid again. Like quick flashes of light, images of my childhood began jumping through my mind's third eye and I saw myself scrolling through photos in albums and on Instagram. I thought about my days in Little League. I thought about my high school presidential speech, wearing my dad's New York Giants Willie Mays jersey. I thought about my first game after joining the JCC softball team and pulling my hamstring after my first at bat of the season. I thought about John Fogerty's "Centerfield." In my mind, I could almost hear the chorus of his song playing in surround sound in my head, "Put me in coach, I'm ready to play. Look at me, I can be, centerfield."

As you would expect of the Baseball Gods, I just happened to be wearing my dad's Willie Mays jersey that day. Channeling my inner Willie Mays, I trotted out to center field with the smile of a little kid on my face. I loved every minute playing in the Blaze scrimmage and I even made a few good defensive plays. Not too shabby for a middle-aged man in flip flops.

Toward the end of practice, Nate came up to the plate for his last at bat of the game. He was already four for four on the day and was looking for his 5th hit. Nate patiently waited and let a few bad pitches thrown by Coach Wright go by. Then he locked in on a fastball right down the middle, and just like all good hitters do when they guess right on a pitch, Nate swung and crushed the ball to deep left center field. The towering fly ball forced the center fielder to make a long run before he jumped in the air and made a back-handed catch that would have made Willie Mays proud. That's when I realized that I had just robbed my own son of a home run.

Having caught the last out of the game, I trotted in from center field with the baseball still in my glove. As I approached Coach Wright in the infield, he said to me, "Hey, you're pretty good, you look young enough, I think you could play for us." I laughed, gently tossed the ball back to him, and replied, "I'd be glad to play for your guys anytime. Just put me in coach, I'm ready to play." I suspect, the only person at the Blaze scrimmage who might have been disappointed with me playing center field that day was my own son Nate.

The Blaze team had a cast of characters worthy of the The Sandlot. Just like in that classic movie, many of the kids on the team had nicknames. First, their catcher, Brady, was nicknamed "Pudge" by his parents in honor of the Boston Red Sox Hall of Fame catcher Carlton Fisk. Pudge even wore #27 on his Blaze jersey, just like Fisk. Then, there was pitcher and first baseman Nick, who was nicknamed "Big Dog" because one of the parents would frequently yell out during his at bats, "Big Dog's got to eat!" Then, there was a kid called "Country Club" by Coach Wright because he once brought a golf club to baseball practice. Ian, the Blaze second baseman, somehow earned the affectionate nickname "Squirtle" from his teammates. Strangely, no one seemed to know what "Squirtle" meant or how Ian got stuck with that nickname. A few days after becoming a member of the Blaze, in recognition of some great plays at short stop during practice, a group of dads gave Nate the nickname "Scoop."

The culture of the Blaze team was cultivated by its team leader and head coach, Dean Wright, who I think would make a great character in a movie. His skin was tan and tough like leather from years of playing and coaching baseball outdoors in Kansas City's hot summer sun. His hair was salty grey, and he had a thick 1970's style mustache that Rollie Fingers, famous for his handlebar mustache, would have been proud of. Coach Wright used slang for every baseball term in the book. He had countless baseball stories to tell, and he always had a valuable lesson to teach.

Coach Wright was also superstitious and frequently mentioned baseball Karma. For example, if the Blaze lost a game, the team would always switch jerseys for the next game. However, if the team won a game, the players would continue to wear the same color jerseys until the winning streak ended. Even though the kids knew the drill, Coach Wright always sent a pre-game email to the team which read something like, "We won yesterday so we will wear the same visiting team jerseys again, even though we are the home team."

Coach Wright was also well versed in the ways of the Baseball Gods. He understood both the written and unwritten rules of baseball. I recall one time during a game, I made the mistake of mentioning that the Blaze pitcher was throwing a no-hitter. This is a classic no-no, which jinxed the pitcher, and of course the next batter got a single to ruin the no-hitter. I had broken a cardinal rule of the Baseball Gods. Coach Wright looked straight at me, shook his head in disappointment, acknowledging that I should have known better.

I remember that day as clearly as if it happened yesterday. It was June 10, 2018, a very hot Kansas day, and Nate's team was playing in a tournament. I saw some parents that I knew sitting under a large umbrella with some room to spare. I don't usually like to sit in the same spot for more than an inning at a time while watching Nate play, but the shade of the umbrella was inviting and seemed to be a good place to watch the game and avoid the blistering sun and the heat. The score was 8-0 and the Blaze pitcher, Nathan, was hurling a gem. Up to that point that day, Nathan was unhittable.

Naively, innocently, mistakenly, but loudly, I asked the group of folks that I was sitting with, "Is Nathan throwing a no-hitter?" One of the mothers looked at me with a surprised, perhaps shocked, look on her face. Realizing what I had just done, I looked up at the sky, put my hands in a prayer formation and said out loud, "Oh my god, I am the author of *The Baseball Gods are Real*, I should know better. Baseball Gods, I take it back, I am sorry. I did not declare that Nathan was throwing a no-hitter, I just asked if he was throwing a no-hitter." The father sitting behind me tapped me on the shoulder and chimed in, "It's too late, you blew it." And I knew I did.

Well, I relearned a very important lesson that day, the hard way. Not only did Nathan lose his bid for a no-hitter, the opposing team went on to score 13 consecutive runs, the Blaze lost the game, and the team got knocked out of the tournament. When the team gathered around for a post-game talk, I jumped in to apologize before Coach Wright addressed them. When I finished, Coach Wright replied, "Yeah, you did lose the game for us. You can't talk about a no-no!" It was a teaching moment regarding *The Rules of the Baseball Gods*, for the team and for me.

During Nate's first season with the Blaze, I discovered just how far Coach Wright's love of baseball and dedication to the kids and the community extended. Backing up against a street of quaint homes in the town of Raytown, MO, there is a small park with a baseball field hidden from street view. Coach Wright built and maintained that ballfield by himself, for the neighborhood kids and for Blaze practices when no other field is available. In front of a makeshift backstop made out of chicken wire and a random collection of large pieces of metal fence was a beautifully groomed infield and an outfield with natural well-cut green grass. Rather than an outfield fence, there was a small pond. This ballfield was another little piece of baseball heaven.

When I watched Nate play at Coach Wright's baseball field, or when we had a catch there, I always lost track of the time. The kids often just played until the sun went down. Many times, they rotated playing positions and took turns at bat. No scoreboard, no outs, no worrying about making errors, no winning or losing, just playing for the love of the game trying to get better. Sometimes after practice, the kids and the adults all drove to the local Dairy Queen, where Coach Wright generously would buy the boys ice cream to reward them for their hard work.

Nate learned a lot about baseball from Coach Wright during his first season with the Blaze and he really improved as a ballplayer. When Nate looks back on his childhood, I think he will always remember Coach Wright and his ballfield, which we affectionately refer to as our "The *Field of Dreams*."

With the arrival of the summer baseball season, the Blaze started competing in more tournaments against better teams from all over the region. The innocence of those special moments playing at Coach Wright's baseball field slowly disappeared and, as usually happens when the level of competition gets tougher, winning became the priority for the team. Unfortunately, winning also became more important to the parents of the players. It didn't take long for the purity of the game that I still remember from my youth to get washed away like a tornado sweeping through the wheat fields of Kansas. Whatever innocence I believed might still exist completely vanished when the Blaze played its first game at the competitive tournament known as the Hawaiian Hitfest.

Ironically, the Hawaiian Hitfest tournament was originally designed to return the game of baseball back to a low-key, fun experience so many of us older folks remember from our own childhoods. It began with a humble beginning in 2003 with just 4 ballfields, 6 employees, 12 umpires and 18 teams. The vision of its founder, Jeremy McDowell, was to offer a tournament where kids could just be kids, play the game they enjoyed, and hopefully fall deeper in love with the game. Emphasizing a Hawaiian theme, McDowell expected that decorated dugouts and ballfields, with parents wearing funny hats and coconut bras, drinking sweet, fruity drinks, would change the atmosphere from an overly intense to a more festive environment. He wanted this tournament to be different than all the others and bring the focus back to kids simply having fun.

The Hawaiian Hitfest was so unique and so successful that it became one of the most popular tournaments in the Midwest region of the U.S. This small-town baseball event that started with just 18 teams grew into a stunning success over the next 15 years, expanding exponentially to 748 teams, 145 ballfields, roughly 160 employees and 45 umpires. However, as better and better teams came to the tournament over the years, the level of intensity of the games increased. With more intense competitions came more competitive parents. As a result, Jeremy McDowell's plan may have backfired.

As the Blaze season progressed, and in anticipation of upcoming tournament play, the coaches began the process of assigning the players to the eight positions on the field. The kids that coaches believe to be less skilled, and therefore didn't earn a starting position, ended up on the bench. These bench players got less playing time in the field, fewer at-bats at the plate, and tended to be more nervous and tentative when they were inserted into the lineup. During Nate's first tournament game at the Hawaiian Hitfest, a parent of a Blaze player noticed that his son was benched again, as was often the case during the regular season. Apparently, the kid's father was getting more and more upset, and more and more vocal on the sidelines, about his son's lack of playing time. Like a tea kettle on a hot stove about to boil over, the temperature began to rise to an extreme level. I could see that it was just a matter of time before the situation exploded.

After their time at bat, Nate and his Blaze teammates had trotted out onto the field. The parent of the perennial bench warmer got up out of his seat in the stands and marched into the Blaze dugout to give the coaches a piece of his mind. He started yelling at them for not playing his son. Coach Wright moved in to try to ease the situation and calm down the irate father. This didn't work. The father pointed and then pressed his finger into Coach Wright's chest and screamed, loud enough for everyone nearby to hear, "I pay you to f%#$ing play my son." The kids still in the dugout at the time were left stunned, as were the parents sitting close by in the stands, including me.

To prevent a fist fight from breaking out between the irate father and Coach Wright, the head umpire, who heard the commotion, intervened. He maneuvered in between the two potential combatants like a Las Vegas boxing referee in a black and white striped shirt. After a short but stern discussion, the angry father was escorted off the field. However, the episode was not over because the father wanted to return to his seat to continue watching the game as if this disturbance had never happened. When the head umpire walked over and politely suggested that he leave the park and cool himself down, the father refused. Now it looked like he was about to start a fight with the head umpire. Just in the nick of time, a police officer walking by came to the aid of the head umpire and defused the situation. He personally escorted the father to the parking lot and told him that he was banned from the game and for the remainder of the tournament as well.

Maybe it was karma or the Baseball Gods at work, but something very positive followed that unfortunate, unpleasant irate parent episode. After the incident, Maryann Maturo, the mom of one of Nate's teammates who saw the whole thing, sent an email to the team with *The Matheny Manifesto* as an attachment. Mike Matheny, best known for the time he was the manager of the St. Louis Cardinals, is also held in high esteem in the Little League world for this manifesto. Many years ago, when Matheny was coaching a competitive youth baseball team, he wrote a frankly worded letter to the parents of the team and it became an internet sensation. He penned a tough love philosophy, essentially a behavioral playbook for players and parents to follow, and it became *The Matheny Manifesto*.

According to the manifesto, Matheny expects hustle, humility, discipline and respect from the players. For the parents, Matheny says that the biggest role they can play is to be a silent source of encouragement. He doesn't embrace parents who constantly yell at their kids, "Come on, let's go, you can do it," which he believes just adds more pressure on them. He strongly suggests that the best way for parents to help their children's development as baseball players is to spend time with them by playing catch, throwing batting practice and hitting them ground balls. I suspect Matheny's manifesto would apply as well to other activities of children, not just baseball.

Nate and I love to play catch and have done so from the time he was old enough to hold a ball in his little hands and toss it to me. For years now, ever since I can remember, we have both daydreamed about the chance to someday have a catch on a professional baseball field. During the summer of 2018, our wish came true.

CHAPTER SEVENTEEN

The Field of Dreams

"Is this heaven? No it's Iowa"
—Ray and Jon Kinsella, *Field of Dreams*

WHEN I THINK OF MY FAVORITE MOVIES, *THE NATURAL*, *Star Wars*, *Indiana Jones*, *E.T.*, *Vacation*, *Bull Durham* and *Major League* come to mind. However, at the end of the day, *Field of Dreams* gets the nod as my all-time favorite. This 1989 American sports fantasy-drama, directed by Phil Alden Robinson with a truly outstanding cast including Kevin Costner, Amy Madigan, James Earl Jones, Ray Liotta and Burt Lancaster, tells the story of an Iowa farmer named Ray Kinsella, played by Costner. In the beginning of the film, Kinsella hears a mysterious voice in his head repeating the phrase over and over again, "If you build it, he will come." At first, he is confused and upset because no one else can hear it. After several additional mysterious vocal messages and events, he becomes convinced that he needs to tear down a large part of the corn field on his farm, which provides his livelihood and his family's safety net, and replace it with a baseball field, even though everyone thinks it's a crazy idea.

Kinsella, against all odds, moves forward with his plan and builds the baseball field in his backyard. Shortly thereafter, the ghosts of seven of the members of the 1919 Chicago White Sox team suddenly appear and come to play ball every day. Just like in *The Sandlot*, they don't have enough players to complete two teams but they play anyway, just for the love of the game. As was the case with the mysterious voice, at first Ray is the only person who can see the ghosts.

However, as in all great movies, the plot thickens. We learn that Kinsella's father used to play baseball in the minor leagues as a young adult. We learn that as a child, his favorite baseball player was Shoeless Joe Jackson. We learn that during the infamous 1919 World Series, in what has become known as the Chicago Black Sox Scandal, several players from the Black Sox, including Shoeless Joe, were accused of being paid by the notorious gangster, Arnold Rothstein, to purposely play poorly and lose so gamblers could make a fortune betting on the games. While Jackson did admit to taking the bribe, there was no evidence that he did anything to purposely lose any games. In fact, Jackson performed very well during the series. We also learn that Ray and his father had a strained relationship and were estranged at the time of the father's death.

At first, Kinsella thought he was building the baseball field for the ghost of Shoeless Joe Jackson. However, late one afternoon, after the ghost baseball players were done for the day, the rookie catcher takes off his mask to introduce himself to Kinsella and thank him for letting them use his field every day. Ray realizes that the young catcher is the ghost of his estranged father. In one of the best, most emotional scenes in movie history, Ray and the ghost of his dead father have a catch under the twinkling lights on their *field of dreams*. If you haven't seen *Field of Dreams*, I suggest you do so. At the very least, you should watch this film's famous 6-minute YouTube video entitled "Playing Catch." I tear up every time I watch it and I'll be surprised if it doesn't have the same effect on you.

Field of Dreams has become an American cinema classic, and rightfully so. The location of the film site has been preserved and has become a popular tourist attraction. Just as predicted in the movie, baseball lovers from across the country come from far and wide to visit this baseball promised land located in the small town of Dyersville, Iowa. Recently, to the surprise of all, Major League Baseball announced that a regular season game between the New York Yankees and the Chicago White Sox will be played right next to the *field of dreams* next year.

On the subject of Iowa, one day I was looking at the summer schedule for the Colorado Springs Sky Sox and noticed that the team would be playing a four-game series in late June against the Iowa Cubs in Des Moines, just a few hour's drive from Kansas City. I was thinking a trip to Des Moines would be another opportunity to see Jon Perrin pitch. I confirmed with Reggie that we had no family plans for that weekend and began making travel arrangements for another father-son adventure.

During the planning process, I mentioned to Nate that the actual *field of dreams* that was used in the movie *Field of Dreams* is located in Dyersville, Iowa, only three hours away from Des Moines. I told Nate that if he wanted to, we would find the time to drive there and have our most memorable catch of all time. I suggested that we depart for Des Moines Thursday morning, get settled in, and attend the Sky Sox/ Cubs ball game that night. Then, first thing Friday morning, we would drive to Dyersville, see the *field of dreams*, take in the atmosphere and its importance, and head back in time for Friday night's game. On Saturday, we would stay in Des Moines for a third game before driving back home to Kansas City. Nate liked the plan, but we were so busy when we got to Des Moines, we never made it to Dyersville.

During the week before this road trip was scheduled to begin, a few things occurred which changed its dynamic. First, catcher Dustin Houle, Perrin's good friend, got called up from Double A-Biloxi to Triple A-Colorado Springs and he would be with the Sky Sox in Des Moines. Second, Jorge Lopez, Perrin's friend and fellow pitcher, was sent down to Triple-A by the Milwaukee Brewers and he too would be with the team in Des Moines. Finally, just days before the trip, Perrin phoned to tell me that he had been sent back down to Double A-Biloxi and we would not be seeing him in Des Moines. I was very surprised and disappointed to hear this. Nevertheless, arrangements were in place, so Nate and I decided to forge ahead with our plans.

Every baseball player follows his own unique road to the show. Dustin Houle's began in Penticton, British Columbia in Canada where he was born and raised. As one would expect of a Canadian kid, he is an avid hockey fan and his favorite team is and has always has been the Vancouver Canucks. Houle also loved baseball, excelled at it, and in 2011was drafted right out of high school by the Milwaukee Brewers in the eighth round.

Houle climbed the baseball ranks and developed a reputation for playing strong defense. He also gained a reputation for toughness, as he overcame several injuries in the early part of his career. Before he even played his first game in the minor leagues, Houle broke the hamate bone in his left hand, underwent surgery, and sat out his first professional baseball season. Houle bounced back the next season as a rookie and moved up to Class-A Wisconsin in 2013.

Just when Houle got healthy and started moving forward on his road to the show, he suffered several additional setbacks. In the offseason, he herniated a disc during a weight training session. After rehabbing his back, a foul tip broke his right thumb during a spring training game. Having recovered from his broken right thumb, he injured his right elbow on his throwing arm requiring "Tommy John" surgery. Next came a torn hamstring. These injuries forced Houle to miss the rest of the season, the second time he had to miss an entire season due to injury. Perhaps this series of injuries was a test by the Baseball Gods.

After five significant injuries over a relatively short period of time, it would be understandable for a player to lose his positive attitude, lose hope and detour off of his road to the show. However, Dustin Houle, like many great athletes in all sports, has something that can't be measured on a stat sheet, no matter how many algorithms the sabermetric experts run in the front office. He has desire, willpower and determination.

Houle was healthy again in 2015 and played for the Class-A Brevard County Manatees. The next season he got promoted to the Double-A Biloxi Shuckers where his play impressed coaches and staff to such an extent, he received an invitation to major league spring training in the Arizona Cactus League in 2017. It was Houle's time to get a taste of big-league life and his road to the show appeared to be back on track.

Houle first met Jon Perrin after Perrin signed his contract with the Milwaukee Brewers. Their friendship blossomed years later when they were roommates during the 2017 season playing together with the Biloxi Shuckers. Catchers, like Houle, and pitchers, like Perrin, have a unique relationship and it is common for those position players to become close friends. It makes sense, since pitchers and catchers spend so much time together. Good chemistry on the field tends to lead to good chemistry off the field. While Perrin often pitched to catcher Jacob Nottingham, a top Brewers' prospect, he seemed to get matched up with Houle the most.

Houle played that full season with the Double-A Biloxi Shuckers and earned another invitation to join the big-league club in Cactus League spring training in 2018. In an article written by Tom Haudricourt in the *Milwaukee Journal Sentinel*, "Houle Turned Heads in Brewers Camp This Spring," Houle says of his injury-riddled past, "It's been a grind. It kind of makes you who you are." I have a feeling that Houle passed the test given by the Baseball Gods and has earned their respect. In 2018, Dustin Houle was selected to join the Canadian national baseball beam.

After having been on the same roster with the Biloxi Shuckers the prior season, Houle and Perrin were now playing together for the Triple-A Colorado Springs Sky Sox. A few days after Perrin's call up to Triple-A, he came in to relief pitch while Houle was catching and together they finished out the game, with Perrin earning a save. It was just like old times for these two when they played together for the Shuckers. They hugged, back slapped and then celebrated the win with their teammates.

In Houle's short time with the Triple-A Colorado Springs Sky Sox, he batted .400 and hit a home run. Unfortunately for him, the Brewers were flooded with catchers, with five on the Sky Sox roster. As a result, by the time Nate and I arrived in Des Moines, Houle was relegated to the role of bullpen catcher. 2018 was a crazy year for Houle on his road to the show. All in the same year, he played in Single-A, Double-A and Triple-A, and ended up in the bullpen.

As Nate and I drove north to Iowa, Perrin was driving south to Biloxi, Mississippi. On our drive, I truly enjoyed seeing the beautiful rolling hills and small towns of northern Missouri miles north of Kansas City. I imagined how peaceful life must be in all of the similar small farm towns across middle America. Quite a difference from hustle and bustle of big city life.

Nate and I arrived in Des Moines hours later after a very pleasant drive that seemed shorter than it was. We toured for a while and discovered it to be an absolutely lovely, charming city. The Des Moines River, a tributary of the mighty Mississippi, runs through it, with bridges crossing over it throughout, giving the city a unique personality.

Iowa, Kansas and Missouri, often called "fly-over" states, do not seem to get the attention or appreciation they deserve, particularly by folks born and raised on the east and west coasts who have never seen them or lived there. I must admit that, as a New Yorker, I had a similar view before I visited Kansas City to meet Reggie's family for the first time. I found

Kansas City to be a wonderful place to visit and live, with its busy, gentrified downtown area, the beautiful Country Club Plaza, especially during the holidays when the Plaza lights brighten the sky, with suburbs that rival those in New York and California. After only a short time in the city, I felt that Des Moines and Kansas City had a lot in common.

Des Moines is the capital of Iowa and the State Capitol building, with its golden dome, is located in the heart of the city. While imposing to see up close, I was more impressed to be able to see the building's gold dome from directly behind home plate at Principal Park, the home of the Iowa Cubs, the Triple-A affiliate of the Chicago Cubs.

I was equally impressed to learn that fans who attend a ballgame at Principal Park on a Saturday can play catch on the field before the game. Nate and I joked that this was the work of the Baseball Gods and our dream of having a catch on a professional baseball field was about to come true.

Nate and I arrived at Principal Park early Friday night, baseball gloves in hand, and scouted the stadium for its ballhawking potential. While we loved the stadium and its vibe, it was not ideal for hawking balls from a batting practice perspective. However, Nate remained optimistic and after batting practice was cancelled due to rain, he concluded that the best place to sit during the game would be next to the Sky Sox bullpen, since it was located right alongside the right field foul line. The players literally sit with their backs right up against the railing of the front row seats.

When the Sky Sox pitchers and catchers arrived in the bullpen area, Dustin Houle recognized me in the stands and came over to say hello. After the bullpen players settled in and did their pre-game handshake ritual, I was able to get the attention of veteran Tim Dillard. We shook hands and I introduced him to Nate. After Dillard went back to his seat at the end of the row of bullpen chairs, I remembered that I had with me the chapter I had written about him, including excerpts from our interview. I had promised to get a copy to him for his approval before this book was published. So, before the game started, I gave the envelope with the chapter to Houle, who was sitting down right in front of us, to pass along to Dillard. When he received it, Dillard gave me a look of acknowledgement and put the envelope in his back pocket.

Nate did not get to hawk balls during batting practice, but the Baseball Gods delivered for him anyway. As it turned out, sitting just above the bullpen was ballhawk heaven. First, Houle tossed Nate a ball. Then Nate asked Jorge Lopez, who was sitting right in front of us to sign that ball. While Lopez was signing, Nate told him that his good friend, Jon Perrin, was teaching him how to pitch back in Kansas City. Lopez looked up from signing the baseball and gave Nate a big smile of recognition.

The next day we arrived at the stadium and batting practice was almost over. Like an experienced ballhawk, Nate ran straight to the right field bleachers to try to get a toss-up ball from one of the players on the field. When Nate arrived at his spot, he noticed Houle and Lopez talking to each other while shagging fly balls further away in center field. Nate greeted them by yelling out, "Hello Mr. Houle, hello Mr. Lopez!" The next ball was hit to deep right center field and Lopez ambled over and made a great catch. He turned around to find Nate in the bleacher section and he threw the ball directly to him.

Nate made the catch, gave Lopez a thumbs up, and screamed "Thank you Mr. Lopez" to show his gratitude.

For three games in a row, Nate and I sat behind the Sky Sox bullpen. By the end of the weekend, we felt like we were part of the team. We got to watch Houle warm up all of the bullpen pitchers, including Lopez and future Milwaukee Brewer Corbin Burnes, throughout each game. We enjoyed Dillard cracking jokes with fellow veteran pitcher Mike Zagurski, now a free agent. We also witnessed some funny moments. During one mid-inning activity primarily for the benefit of the fans in the stands, the stadium staff blasted packaged hot dogs out of a cannon. Some shots misfired toward the Sky Sox bullpen. All of the Sky Sox pitchers and catchers jumped in the air, like hungry birds, to snag a hot dog. Lopez caught one using a basketball box-out move to outmaneuver his teammates and quickly scarfed down the hot dog. Then, another hot dog landed at the far end of the bullpen near veterans Dillard and Zagursky. Clearly, both wanted the hotdog but neither seemed inclined to wrestle over it like the younger guys just had. So, they settled things like gentleman and agreed to share it, with each taking a bite and passing it on until it was gone. It was a funny and heartwarming moment.

That Saturday at Principal Park was a day Nate and I will remember forever. We got the opportunity to fulfill one of our long-time father-son dreams, to have a catch on the field of a professional baseball team. In anticipation of this unforgettable experience, we even had a "practice" catch outside of the stadium before the gates opened. As soon as we were allowed in, Nate raced onto the field like a thoroughbred racehorse who had just broken out of the starting gate. When he ran far enough into the outfield to realize that he was free and clear, he took a deep breath and spread his arms out wide, looked towards the sky, and thanked the Baseball Gods. Stepping on a professional minor league field for the first time to have a catch with his dad was a very special moment for Nate. It was as if he knew that this day was a temporal marker on his own road to the show.

When I finally caught up to Nate in center field, we marveled at the perfectly cut outfield grass and the smooth-as-silk dirt in the infield we had passed on the way. We were both surprised to see how tall the outfield walls were and how wide the view seemed from our position in the outfield. I'm sure Nate was picturing himself playing center field, making a great jumping catch off the wall and throwing the ball to the cutoff man, just like Willie Mays used to do when he played in the Polo Grounds in New York.

After we viewed the stadium outfield and took in the atmosphere, Nate and I knew it was the perfect time to have our long-awaited father-son catch. We warmed up with some easy tosses, lengthening the distance between us with each throw. Eventually, we were throwing from center field all the way into right field. Then, just like we always did on our driveway at home, we moved on to pop flies and ground balls. We simply could not stop smiling, playing catch on our *field of dreams*. We had manifested this moment and knew it. It was the best and most enjoyable catch that we'd ever had. When the event organizer announced over the loudspeaker system that there was only five minutes left to play catch, Nate and I came together with shorter tosses to end our catch the same way we had started it. When we finished and stood together,

I channeled Ray Kinsella's father from *Field of Dreams* and asked Nate, "Is this Heaven?" Nate replied with a big smile, "No, it's Iowa."

Our trip to Des Moines ended on a high note and Nate and I talked about that fabulous weekend all the way home in the car. We agreed that the only missing piece was Jon Perrin. However, we did get to see Perrin when he returned to Kansas City during the Biloxi Shockers all-star break. During his visit, we discussed his recent demotion from Triple-A to Double-A, despite his having solid pitching statistics while in the upper league. Perrin simply replied, "It's a business," something my dad always said about professional sports. Perrin explained that the Milwaukee Brewers had a few pitchers coming off the disabled list and, as a result, he was getting moved down to make room for some veterans. Actually, that made sense. Then we made plans to go to a yoga class and Kayla and Nate agreed to join us. It was the first time Perrin did yoga with me and both of my kids.

CHAPTER EIGHTEEN

The Natural

"Fred, it took me 16 years to get here. You play me,
and you'll get the best I've got."
—Roy Hobbs, *The Natural*

AS I MENTIONED PREVIOUSLY, *FIELD OF DREAMS* IS MY favorite movie of all time. *The Natural*, another baseball movie released in 1984 based on the novel with the same name, is a close second. The movie, directed by Barry Levinson, with a great cast including Robert Redford, Glenn Close and Robert Duvall, takes place in the 1950s. Like the book, the film recounts the experiences of Roy Hobbs, a quiet country boy with great "natural" baseball talent.

At the beginning of the movie, a young Hobbs is seen playing ball with his father on the family farm. During their father-son catch, his dad gives him the following important advice. He says, "You've got a gift Roy, but it's not enough. You've got to develop yourself." Unfortunately for Hobbs, that was the last piece of advice he ever received from his father.

Later that day, Hobbs' father dies of an apparent heart

attack working in the backyard of their farmhouse. As Hobbs hugs his father on the ground under a tree, the sky begins to rumble in the distance. That night during the fierce rainstorm, the tree in the backyard is struck by lightning and is split in half. After the storm moves on, Hobbs decides to honor his father by carving a baseball bat from the broken tree. He burns a picture of a lightning bolt on the barrel of the bat and names the bat "Wonderboy." When I first watched this movie as a kid, I didn't capture the symbolism of that scene. It did not occur to me then, but I realize now, that his father's spirit was with Hobbs every time he used that baseball bat.

Hobbs overcomes the loss of his father and embarks on his promising baseball career. However, as 19-year old on his way to a tryout with the Chicago Cubs, he is shot by an obsessed, unstable, crazed baseball fan and his baseball career is abruptly halted. Hobbs would have to wait 16 years before he would return to his road to the show.

Fast forward those 16 long years. Hobbs, now a grown man who should be close to retirement, enters professional baseball as a 35-year old rookie for the last-place New York Knights. Initially, Hobbs rides the bench and argues about playing time with the Knight's manager, Pop Fisher. Finally, after the losses keep piling up, Pop gives Hobbs a chance to play. To everyone's surprise, Hobbs' play is outstanding, with him hitting home runs game after game. Hobbs becomes one of the best players in the league and the Knights become a winning team.

Of course, *The Natural* is part fantasy and all Hollywood. In the climactic scene, an injured, bleeding Hobbs comes to the plate, with lightening flashing in the sky, for what will be his last at bat as a professional baseball player. And what does he do? He smashes the game-winning home run deep to right field into the lights above the upper deck of the stadium. Hobbs' home run smash causes a fireworks display that would rival a celebration on the 4th of July.

The Natural left a deep impression on me as a kid and apparently it had a big impact on many other film and baseball fans as well. The legacy of the baseball movie classic lives on thanks to the Kansas City Royals, who named their Northwest Arkansas Double-A affiliate the Naturals. To further associate their team with the movie, the Naturals baseball cap insignia is the letter N, created out of a bolt of lightning. From the time I learned that Jon Perrin was a professional baseball player with the Milwaukee Brewers organization, I tried to manifest a Brewers/Royals trade that would bring him to Kansas City. In my manifestations, Perrin would make his Royals' debut after the trade pitching for the Naturals.

Over the next several months, I chatted up Perrin to my neighbor Dayton Moore, the General Manager of the Royals. My intention, to impress upon Moore that Perrin, a local kid from Olathe, KS, would be a real asset to the team and to the community.

The first time I spoke to Moore about Perrin was opening day of the minor league season in late March 2017. I had just finished a meditation session on my backyard deck, opened my eyes, and saw Moore sweeping off his backyard porch. I strolled over and we talked at length. During our conversation, I spoke about my blossoming relationship with Perrin and told Moore that he would be a great fit for the Royals organization.

My next conversation with Moore on this subject occurred

a few months later in August. On a power walk in the neighborhood, I happened to see Moore in his car as he was pulling out of his driveway. He pulled over to the side and stopped to chat. Coincidentally, Nate had just completed a week session at Moore's summer baseball camp and he was anxious to talk about Nate's experience. Nate had earned the MVP award for his group and Moore said he was really proud of Nate and pleased with his progress. I told Moore how much Nate loved camp and that he was already looking forward to baseball camp again next year. Changing the subject, I mentioned that the Royals had just called up infielder Roman Torres from its Triple-A Omaha affiliate and assigned number 46 as his jersey number. Since Perrin's favorite jersey number is 46, I joked that after the Royals traded for Perrin, he and Torres would have to work something out. Before Moore pulled away in his car, I asked if his scouts were still looking at Perrin. Moore smiled and nodded his head with a confirming yes.

My next contact with Moore regarding Perrin was not a conversation. It was a written scouting report I provided in December in anticipation of the upcoming baseball winter meetings a few days away. The winter meetings are notorious for off-season trades. It makes sense, since every General Manager in both leagues is at the same place at the same time. The meetings even have a nickname, the "Hot Stove Season." Back in the day, the GMs would meet in hotel rooms in the cold winter months in New York City and talk trades sitting around a hot stove to keep warm. Now, the annual winter meetings are held in warm places like Orlando or Las Vegas. I guess modern day GMs know what they're doing.

In preparation for the winter meetings, I created my own

scouting report about Perrin for Moore to read before he left town. I put every article and public scouting report I could find about Perrin into a folder and added a cover letter that read, "Dear Dayton, Good luck at the winter meetings. May the Baseball Gods be with you. Warm regards, Jonathan Fink." I sealed the envelope and dropped it off at his house.

I also tried a manifesting experiment to facilitate a trade. I went to Scheels, a local sporting goods store in Overland Park, and ordered a grey Royals visiting team jersey. I had the jersey custom-made with "Perrin 46" sewn on the back. I hoped wearing that jersey during the time of the winter meetings would be send a message to the Baseball Gods that I wanted Perrin traded from the Brewers to the Royals. That didn't happen, but I wore my new Perrin 46 jersey to nearly every Royals game I went to the next season.

Months later, at the start of the 2018 season, I felt a surge in purpose and motivation to get Perrin traded to the Royals. Circumstances seemed to be in my favor. The Milwaukee Brewers looked playoff bound, stacked with talented major league pitchers and backed up with solid minor league pitchers as well. On the other hand, the Royals, with the second worst record in the American League and a relatively weak pitching staff, had just begun the process of rebuilding the team. Was there a better place for Perrin now than in Kansas City with the Royals?

During the course of the season, additional circumstances developed that supported my manifestation. As expected, the Brewers were making a run for the playoffs and David Stearns, their General Manager, was looking to trade prospects for established veterans to add a few missing pieces to a potential

World Series team. The Royals, now rebuilding in earnest, were looking to trade some of their veterans for younger players and prospects. In one transaction, the Royals traded veteran pitcher Kelvin Herrera, who had been with the team since 2011, to the Washington Nationals for three minor league prospects. In another transaction, just before the trade deadline, the Royals sent veteran third baseman Mike Moustakas to the Brewers for outfielder Brett Phillips and pitching prospect Jorge Lopez. Yes, the same Jorge Lopez who signed a ball for Nate when we visited Des Moines and later tossed him another ball from the bullpen and the same Jorge Lopez who Jon Perrin warmed up with before his Cactus League debut with the Brewers.

Initially, right after the trade, the Royals assigned Lopez to the team's Triple-A affiliate in Omaha to give him the opportunity and experience to prove himself as a starting pitcher. After his third start, he was called up to the show and Nate and I planned to be at Kauffman Stadium for his Royals debut. We were astonished by the fact that Lopez and Phillips were playing for the Triple-A Sky Sox in Iowa just a few weeks ago. Now both were scheduled to be in that day's starting lineup, not just in the major leagues, but for our own Kansas City Royals. We acknowledged this surreal development and said almost at the exact same time, "The Baseball Gods are Real!"

It may have been karma, but after the Lopez/Phillips trade, I decided to test the law of attraction and celebrate. I went to Scheels sporting goods store again and bought a new Jorge Lopez Royals jersey. I also bought a #14 Brett Phillips jersey as a gift for Nate for making the Kansas All-State team. I knew Nate would really appreciate this jersey for three reasons. First, he loves to wear baseball jerseys just like I do. Second, he had a ball Brett Phillips had signed for him in his baseball collection at home, the one I had given to him when I returned home from spring training in Arizona in February. Third, Phillips and Nate both wear the same jersey number, #14.

Wearing our Royals Lopez and Phillips jerseys, Nate and I arrived early at Kauffman Stadium in anticipation of Lopez's pitching debut and headed straight to the bullpen to watch him warm up. We hoped to get the chance to say hello to him, welcome him to Kansas City, and wish him good luck. Lopez recognized us, walked over, and we got to do all of the things we had hoped to do.

After we said goodbye to Lopez and started to walk to our seats for the game, I was approached by a woman with her daughter. She told me her name was Emily and that she worked for David Glass, the owner of the Royals. She said that Mr. Glass noticed Nate and me wearing our Phillips and Lopez jerseys and wanted to give us two tickets to Diamond Club seats to thank us for supporting the Royals and being such loyal fans. Surprised and pleased, I thanked her and Mr. Glass for the tickets. Before we parted ways, I mentioned that my book about baseball and spirituality was scheduled for release the following week and this encounter with her was an amazing wink from the universe. Then I told her that the Baseball Gods are definitely real. Despite all the good vibes that day, the Toronto Blue Jays defeated the Royals 6-5 and Jorge Lopez took the loss.

I hadn't seen my good neighbor, Dayton Moore, in a while but a few days later, I literally ran into him on my morning jog. We talked about our families and baseball and I mentioned that my first book was just about to be released. Moore asked me how Nate was doing and I told him that he had been invited to join the U12 Kansas All-State team and would be playing with and against 13-year old kids for the fall baseball season. Lastly, I mentioned that I thought the recent trade with the Brewers was a step in the right direction for the Royals. I said that the only problem with the deal was that there was a player missing, Jon Perrin. This chance meeting gave me an opportunity to provide Moore with an update on Perrin's successful season in the minor leagues. Our chat finished, we shook hands and said good-bye. While walking away, I turned back to him and said, "Please trade for my boy!" Moore replied, "I will."

After that conversation with Dayton Moore, I was hopeful that another trade with the Brewers would be announced, one including Jon Perrin. However, the trade deadline came and went. I remained optimistic that a trade for Perrin might get done next season, or perhaps the Royals would select him in the upcoming Rule 5 Draft, since Perrin was now eligible.

For those not familiar with inner workings of back office baseball, the Rule 5 Draft is a special draft that takes place during the winter meetings. Basically, any player that has been drafted and signed by a team and has not been called up to the major leagues after six seasons is eligible to be drafted by another team, provided that team agrees to keep that player on their 40-man roster during the upcoming season. If the team that makes the Rule 5 selection decides they no longer want to keep that player on their 40-man roster, they must return the player to his original team.

Baseball has other back office strategies that permit teams to make trades after the official end of the trade deadline. For example, players that have been designated for assignment or cut by their team, rather than clearing waivers and becoming free agents, are eligible to be traded after the trade deadline. Also, league rules permit minor league players to be traded for other minor league players, with limited restriction. It was this last rule that made my dream come true. On August 7, 2018, Dayton Moore traded Royals minor league pitcher Sal Biasi to the Milwaukee Brewers for Jon Perrin. I was in awe of the work of the Baseball Gods and, over and over in my mind I said to myself, they are definitely real.

The Royals were eager to see what they had in Jon Perrin so they scheduled him to make his debut as the starting pitcher for *the Natural*s just two days later against the Midland RockHounds, the Oakland Athletics' Double-A affiliate. Once again Perrin packed his bags, got in his car, and drove to another new city that he would call home for an unknown period of time. This time Perrin drove north from Biloxi, Mississippi to Arvest Ballpark in Springdale, Arkansas. Since it was August and Nate was still on summer vacation from school, off we went on another father-son adventure driving south from Leawood to the lovely town of Springdale.

With three hours and 200 hundred miles behind us, Nate and I arrived at Arvest Ballpark very early before game time. Within minutes Nate was hunting for balls. However, *the Natural*s' ballpark is not ideal for ballhawking because the stadium has a restaurant that sits behind the left field wall. Home run balls hit over the left field wall land in an open, outdoor picnic table area. When Nate discovered this area of the stadium, he found a bunch of baseballs all over the ground just waiting for him. This was easy pickings and once again Nate was in ballhawk heaven.

On this warm, partly cloudy day in Arkansas, Perrin was going to pitch in the first game of a double header, with Nick Dini behind the plate as his catcher. We excitedly looked on while Perrin made his warmup throws. This was the first time Nate got to see Perrin pitch in a real game and he did not disappoint. Perrin made it through the first three innings without giving up a hit. Nate and I looked at each other but neither mentioned it. After completing five innings of work, Perrin was taken out of the game and we gave him a standing ovation. Perrin had a terrific debut as a Royal.

After the game ended, Nate and I went over to *the Natural*s' dugout to say hello to Perrin and congratulate him on his great performance. A few minutes later, he went into the locker room to hit the showers and we started walking back to our seats for the second game of the doubleheader. On our way, an employee of *the Natural*s tapped Nate on the shoulder and asked him if he wanted to be the team bat boy for the next game, which is something Nate has always wanted to do. I knew this was another Baseball Gods moment when my very happy, excited, son said yes, with a truly picture worthy smile on his face.

Nate had the time of his life as a bat boy, hanging out in the dugout with the coaches and players. He ate sunflower seeds, chewed a huge wad of gum, and watched the interactions of the coaches and players. Seeing handshakes, watching players patting each other on the back after a good play, hearing the words of encouragement the players were giving each other, Nate could feel the positive vibrations in the dugout. When *the Natural*s were up to bat, Nate took great pride in his bat boy responsibilities and was pleased to hear praise from the players. Clearly, this was a day Nate will remember for a long time.

Right there, on a warm, cloudy August day at Arvest Ballpark in Springdale, Arkansas, the Baseball Gods made two baseball dreams come true. Mine, Jon Perrin pitching for the Kansas City Royals organization, and Nate's, being the bat boy for the day.

CHAPTER NINETEEN

The Hank Greenberg Experiment Revisited

"I am confident that there truly is such a thing as living again, that the living spring from the dead, and that the souls of the dead are in existence."
—Socrates

IN MY FIRST BOOK I DESCRIBE MY PARTICIPATION IN WHAT turned out to be a fascinating past life regression session with Kirsten Harwick Mills at Silent Synergy located in my home town of Leawood, Kansas. The objective of this experimental session was to determine whether I was in some way spiritually related to Hank Greenberg, the legendary Jewish baseball player. However, during the session I went back to the 1800s, not to 1938 as initially intended. In a meditative state under hypnosis, my mind's third eye did not see Hank Greenberg hitting home runs at Tiger Stadium in Detroit, Michigan. Instead, I saw a vivid vision of me as a farmer somewhere in Kansas towards the end of the 19th century.

In regression, I saw acres of wheat fields and beyond them sunflower fields as far as the eye could see. I turned around slowly to take in the scenery and my 360-degree view of the farm revealed a log cabin to the right, a small hill to the left, and several groups of bushes and tall trees out in the distance in the sunflower fields. I was not sure if the sun was rising or setting, but the orange color of the sky was breathtaking.

Out of hypnosis after the session, I thought the experiment had failed because it did not achieve its objective. I didn't regress back to 1938 nor did my past life vision relate in any way to Hank Greenberg. However, what I did experience gave me a greater sense that past lives and reincarnation do occur. Little did I know at the time that the vision I saw in regression would resurface months later, not once, but twice.

September 8, 2018 was a very special day. First and most importantly, it was Reggie's birthday. Second, my parents were in town for the weekend to help celebrate with us and Reggie's family. The weekend festivities included Friday and Saturday night family dinners that I arranged and two fun afternoon activities, one on Saturday to the Westport Art Fair, and the other on Sunday to the University of Kansas in Lawrence, KS, co-planned by Kayla and Reggie.

Folks not familiar with Kansas City might not know that it is an outstanding art community. The Nelson-Atkins Museum of Art is a treasure, with its neoclassical architecture and extensive art collection. The annual Country Club Plaza Art Fair is nationally recognized and attracts well known artists from all over the country. The Westport Art Fair, now called Art Westport, is best known for its dedication to local artists and will be celebrating its 40th year next September.

After brunch Saturday morning, off we went as planned to the Westport Art Fair. We casually strolled Westport's pedestrian friendly streets, stopping from time to time to peruse the artwork and jewelry in covered booths, enjoying another beautiful day in Kansas City. One of the highlights of the art fair for me was seeing so many different breeds of dogs being walked by their owners. I was a little jealous that our dogs, Charlie and Buddy, were at home sleeping on the couch rather being here at the art fair with all of us.

As we were leaving the art fair, with the glare of the setting sun catching my eye through the trees in the distance, I turned to my left and a painting in the last booth caught my attention. As I stepped closer to get a better look, I realized that the artist had painted a picture of a scene that looked exactly like the vision of the Kansas farmland I had seen during my past life regression session. I stood in front of this painting for some time in disbelief. I simply could not believe my eyes. In the painting, the sky was bright sunset orange, there were large groups of bushes and tall trees out in the distance on the left and right, and in the middle, as far as the eye could see, were hundreds, perhaps thousands, of beautiful yellow sunflowers. I took a photo of this incredible painting with my iPhone, including the artist's description which said, "*Sunset Glow*" painted in Leavenworth County, Kansas. Was it a coincidence that on the next day of Reggie's birthday weekend, we planned to visit a sunflower field in the city of Lawrence and then go to University of Kansas to tour the school's campus. As fate would have it, both the sunflower field and the KU campus are located in Leavenworth County Kansas.

Another interesting Baseball Gods moment occurred that weekend. After a lovely birthday dinner with my parents and Reggie's extended family, I took out my wallet to get a credit card to pay the bill, grabbed my iPhone, and while waiting for the waiter to return, checked the score of the game the Royals were playing that night. The game was already in the 6th inning and to my amazement, Jorge Lopez was pitching a perfect game against the Minnesota Twins. What was so surprising was that two nights before, attending my most recent Royals game, I brought a few signed copies of *The Baseball Gods Are Real* to the stadium to distribute. When I learned that Lopez was pitching on Saturday night, I decided to give him a signed copy. I wrote a note inside the book cover that said, "Good luck tomorrow. May the Baseball Gods be with you!" and signed my name. I brought the signed copy to the Customer Service desk and arranged for the book to be hand delivered to Lopez.

We got home from Reggie's dinner in time to watch the end of an exciting Royals game as if it was Game 7 of the World Series. After eight innings, Lopez was perfect. Twenty-four batters came to the plate and twenty-four batters were sent back to the dugout. No hits, no walks, no errors, and Lopez became the first pitcher in Royals history to go into the 9th inning with a perfect game. Unfortunately, Lopez walked the first batter in the top of the 9th and the perfect game was gone. Then he gave up a single and the no-hitter was gone. That base hit streaked past Lopez and actually touched his glove on its way into center field. Although Lopez was taken out and did not finish the game, his performance that night was remarkable. As I said, it was a Baseball Gods moment.

The next morning, I awoke early with a sense of excitement. I was really looking forward to our trip to Lawrence. I had a strange feeling that the sunflower field we were going to see would be the same sunflower field I saw in the *Sunset*

Glow painting and also the same field I plowed as a farmer in my past life regression. I decided to recognize this possibility by wearing my white Detroit Tigers Hank Greenberg baseball jersey. I remember saying to Reggie as we piled into our Acura SUV, "If there is a wheat field right next to the sunflower field, this is the place."

After an hour drive, first on highways leaving Leawood and then on country roads on our way to Lawrence, we parked the SUV in the visitor's parking area on the muddy lawn of Grinter's Sunflower Farm in Leavenworth County. We all got out of the car and the first thing I did was look at the landscape in front of me. Sure enough, there it was, a wheat field right next to the sunflower field, with sunflowers stretching in the distance as far as I could see. I stood for several minutes in disbelief. I knew that I had never been to this spot before in my lifetime. Yet, I knew that Grinter's Sunflower Farm looked exactly like sunflower field in *Sunset Glow* and replicated the vision I saw during my past life regression session. Standing there mesmerized, looking at the endless field of sunflowers, I had this sense, this inner knowledge, that I had lived here before as a farmer in a prior life. First the vision, then the painting, and now the visit provided confirmation. Finally, I also knew that the Hank Greenberg experiment was actually a huge success after all.

CHAPTER TWENTY

The Polo Grounds Experiment

"Maybe I was born to play ball. Maybe I truly was."
—Willie Mays

BRUCE SPRINGSTEEN WAS "BORN TO RUN," WILLIE MAYS
was "Born to play ball." Maybe I was born to be a financial
advisor, run my own investment firm, and become an author.
Maybe I truly was. I enjoy helping people with their financial affairs and managing their assets and it is very reward-
ing when a client recommends me and my firm to a friend or
relative. I also enjoyed writing my first book, so much so that
before I even finished it, I was already thinking about getting
it published and writing this sequel. Then, as if the Baseball
Gods were somehow in control of the process, I found videos
on YouTube which educated me about book publishing and,
specifically, self-publishing.

It is well documented that Amazon set in motion a major
change in the retail sales industry and turned it upside down
when the company entered the business of selling books. Now,
with a continually surging stock price, a huge, growing market
capitalization, and the ability to buy almost anything online

in seconds in the comfort of your home, it is easy to forget that, at first, the one and only thing Amazon sold was books. Long before amazon.com offered smart home devices like Echo, with its artificial intelligence and a now famous voice named Alexa, video streaming and music, the website was just an online book retailer. However, Amazon, led by founder and CEO Jeff Bezos, differentiated itself from the competition by mastering supply chain distribution, customer relationship management and, of course, e-commerce. Over time, Amazon developed sophisticated distribution channels on the operations side of the business and rolled out a groundbreaking customer membership program called "Prime," which, among other things, guaranteed free two-day delivery.

The traditional book retailers were not prepared for a company like Amazon and simply could not compete with its vision and innovation. Amazon's entry into the book selling business eventually led to the demise of many small book retailers and even toppled a large one, Borders Books. Barnes & Noble, formerly the leading book retailer, is still in business, but the company's market share has declined steadily over the last decade and its future is in doubt. Personally, I think there is room for both sales outlets because many folks still enjoy strolling the aisles of a bookstore looking for a title that catches their attention. Also, many authors still welcome the opportunity to read chapters of their books to the public at book signings, as I did recently at the Barnes & Noble in Leawood in connection with *The Baseball Gods are Real -Volume 1*.

While Amazon gets credit for dramatically changing the retail book business, I question whether the company gets enough credit for how much it has helped to transform the book publishing industry. CreateSpace, a subsidiary of Amazon, and its peers, such as IngramSpark, Lulu Press and AuthorHouse, have empowered authors all over the world to self-publish their own books. Thanks to a new technology innovation called "POD," or "Printing on Demand," authors can remain independent and can sell books without retaining a literary agent or contracting with a traditional publishing company. Thanks to POD technology, a self-publisher can even sell books without a physical inventory. Using POD's self-publishing business model, a customer can buy a book on amazon.com or another online book seller with just a few clicks on their iPhone or iPad. That book will be immediately printed and mailed out if the purchaser wants a hard copy or paperback. Alternatively, it can be sent electronically if the purchaser wants the book delivered to their Kindle, iPad or computer. No longer is there the burden of physical inventory and the significant cost of storage or shelf space for book publishers. This is a game-changer.

In the good old days, after an author completed writing a book, he or she first needed to find a literary agent. This process could take months, or even years, especially if the author was unable to find a "fit" with an agent or if agents didn't think the author worthy of representation. After the author found an agent willing to sign on, that agent began the grueling process of convincing a book company to publish the author's book and negotiating the size of the first printing. This step in the process could also take months or even years.

On the other hand, self-publishing is a much quicker process and potentially more profitable for aspiring authors than contracting with a traditional book publishing company. In the traditional arrangement, after the agent gets paid and the book publisher gets paid, the author is usually left with a small percentage of the profits. Not only do authors lose a large share of the profits, they also risk losing creative control of their projects. That said, for well-known authors with name recognition and a successful body of work, who have leverage in negotiations, a contract with a large publishing company is often the way to go.

I spent many late nights reading articles and watching educational videos to absorb as much as possible about the risks and benefits of self-publishing. During this endeavor, I learned everything I could about the book publishing process, including book editing, book formatting, book layout and book cover design. Then I focused on marketing, which was easier for me given the MBA I earned at the Henry W. Bloch School of Management at the University of Missouri-Kansas City after graduating from Tulane. I thought back to "the 4 P's" that I learned in business school: product, price, place and promotion. After completing my research, I decided it was in my best interest to self-publish my first book and create my own publishing company.

I knew that in order to establish a publishing company and file the necessary documents, I needed a company name. I thought the name should reflect one of my most import-ant interests, namely family, finance, music or baseball. As if struck by a lightning bolt sent by the Baseball Gods, the answer was right in front of me.

One day, sitting at my dining room table editing the first draft of my first book, I looked at the stack of baseball related books piled high on the other side of the table. The books were arranged in chronological order to reflect the baseball era of the period: the 1920s of Babe Ruth and Lou Gehrig, the 1930s of Hank Greenberg and pitcher Lefty Grove, the 1940s of Ted Williams and Joe DiMaggio. I stopped when I got to the 1950s because I noticed a book about the 1954 World Series and zeroed in on it.

The book, *1954: The Year Willie Mays and the First Generation of Black Superstars Changed Major League Baseball Forever*, written by Bill Madden, stood out because of its bright orange spine. On its cover was a picture of the great Willie Mays making his famous over-the-shoulder catch of the deep fly ball hit off of the bat of Cleveland Indian slugger, Vic Wertz, in Game 1 of the 1954 World Series. Mays made this memorable catch, which some folks believe was the greatest defensive play in baseball history, at his home stadium, the Polo Grounds.

I grabbed that orange and green 1954 World Series book from the pile on the dining room table and started thumbing through its pages. A sense of nostalgia swept over me. I thought about my dad as a kid because Willie Mays was his favorite ballplayer growing up. I thought about my Grandma Sally and Grandpa Norman raising their family in a small apartment in the Bronx. I thought about Grandpa Norman taking my dad to the Polo Grounds as often as he could so my dad could watch Willie Mays play in person. I thought about Lou Gehrig and Hank Greenberg, both of whom had grown up the Bronx. Then it hit me. The name of my publishing company should be "Polo Grounds Publishing." I thought the name was so perfect that I decided to keep it even after I found out that the Polo Grounds was actually located in Upper Manhattan, near, but not in, the Bronx.

The Polo Grounds stood in the shadows of New York City in an area of Upper Manhattan known as Coogan's Bluff, just south and west of the Bronx. The stadium was best known as the home of the New York Giants baseball team until ownership relocated to San Francisco in 1957. Many professional and college football games were played there over the years and, to the surprise of many, both the New York Mets and the New York Yankees called the Polo Grounds home for brief periods of time.

An aerial view of the Polo Grounds would have shown a stadium shaped like a bathtub or a horseshoe, more suited for football than baseball. However, its unique dimensions as a ballpark gave the stadium character and charm. The distance down the baselines to the foul poles measured 279 feet to left field and only 257 feet to right field. These short porches in the corners were ideal for home run hitters that could really pull the ball. The distance to the center field bleachers was 500 feet, one of the deepest in baseball history, turning many fly balls that would have been home runs in other ballparks into routine fly ball outs. At the Polo Grounds, a batter could hit a ball 470 feet to center field for an out and another batter could hit a ball 260 feet down the right filed line for a home run. I guess the Baseball Gods would call that rough justice.

The center field outfield at the Polo Grounds was huge, designed for speedy defensive players like Willie Mays. If a batter really crushed a ball, but it went into the great abyss of straight-away center field, most likely it would be caught. In that legendary photo of Mays making his famous over-the-shoulder catch while running full speed toward the center field wall in the 1954 World Series, Vic Wertz drove the ball a stunning 483 feet away from home plate for an out.

Three years before that great catch by Willie Mays, one of the greatest moments in baseball history took place at the Polo Grounds. On October 3, 1951, the New York Giants hosted their arch rivals, the Brooklyn Dodgers, to determine who would win the National League pennant and face the New York Yankees in the World Series. The Giants had just completed a miracle run to the post season, winning 37 of their final 44 games, catching up to the Dodgers to force a three-game playoff to decide the league championship.

With the playoff series tied 1-1 and the Dodgers ahead 4-2 in the series finale, Giants outfielder Bobby Thompson hit a stunning, game-winning, three-run home run in the bottom of the 9th inning into the left field seats to win the playoff series. Thompson's epic home run was captured, and memorialized, by Giants' announcer Russ Hodges, who hollered as he was broadcasting the game, "There's a long drive ... It's gonna be, I believe ... The Giants win the pennant! The Giants win the pennant! The Giants win the pennant! The Giants win the pennant! Bobby Thompson hits into the lower deck of the left-field stands! The Giants win the pennant and they're going crazy! They're going crazy! ... I don't believe it, I don't believe it." This miracle moment in baseball history, no doubt brought to you by the Baseball Gods, is referred to as "The Shot Heard Round the World."

I suspect few, if any, of my readers were at the Polo Grounds that day to see Thompson's epic home run in person. Most likely they did not see it on television or hear it broadcast on the radio either. If this describes you, I suggest that you visit YouTube to watch this miracle moment captured on video. It will be well worth your time.

Despite the excitement of Thompson's "shot heard round the world" and Willie Mays' great catch in 1951 and 1954, the New York Giants had difficulty as a franchise. The problem was not its seating capacity, which had been increased from 34,000 seats to an impressive 54,000 seats in 1953. As is the case with most modern-day relocations, it came down to money, a new stadium, one publicly financed with adequate parking. During the 1957 season, the National league baseball owners agreed to permit the Giants, and at the same time, the Brooklyn Dodgers, to move to sunny California. In October of that year, after the baseball season had ended, both teams announced their intention to relocate, breaking the hearts of their loyal fans. I believe my dad, who was 11 years old at the time, still hasn't forgiven the Giants. Years later in 1964, the Polo Grounds was demolished and replaced by a public housing project.

My marketing plan for Polo Grounds Publishing targeted four cities where baseball is extremely popular, Kansas City, Milwaukee, Los Angeles and New York. In addition to my marketing efforts, I channeled the Baseball Gods for help. During my daily yoga and meditation sessions, I asked my spirit guides and *guardian* angels for their assistance in promoting my book. When I meditated, I envisioned selling 100 books, then 1,000 books, then 10,000 books, and then 100,000 books. I visualized my book being made into a Hollywood movie and could see the actors who would play the lead roles in the film. I visualized a book review in the local newspaper. I visualized guest interviews on radio and podcasts. I visualized speaking at book stores and at book clubs. I even visualized going on a nationwide book tour. I could see my book as a huge success reaching thousands of people in a positive and helpful way. I was hoping to manifest a successful reality.

It took several weeks to get *The Baseball Gods are Real – Volume 1* from final draft to publication. First, I asked my parents to read the book for context and editing. Then Meg Schader edited the revised version. Then Meg Reid designed the book cover and layout. Then Freek Bouw provided the book cover photo of Jon Perrin, Kim Watson provided my biography photo and Abi Laksono provided the logo for Polo Grounds Publishing. Everyone did a great job and I sincerely thank them. The book was now ready to go and as a first-time author and book publisher, I couldn't have been more anxious or excited.

Immediately thereafter some things occurred to convince me that the Baseball Gods were helping me on this path. During the first week of August, I uploaded my book file to my independent distribution company partner IngramSpark. I set August 22nd as the pre-sale date and August 28th as the official release date. On August 16th, I went online and clicked on amazon.com to check new releases of baseball books, now a nightly ritual for me. Just for kicks, I typed in the search bar "The Baseball Gods are..." and the algorithm, anticipating my next word, added the word "Real." I clicked again and the search engine kicked into high gear. I landed on a webpage that should not have even existed yet. Six days before my book was supposed to be available for purchase on amazon.com, the hardcover was already on pre-sale. The book cover photo was missing but all the other relevant information was there, the price, the number of pages, the publishing company and the book description. The webpage clearly stated that the pre-sale date was August 22nd, yet the book was already on pre-sale. How could this be? Did the Baseball Gods go into cyberspace to launch my book early?

I thought this was a strange, one-off anomaly until I went to the Barnes & Noble website and saw that my book was on pre-sale there as well. Even more bizarre, the website had my hardcover copy already on sale, without my permission, at a slight discount off of the full retail price. I was certainly surprised to see things moving so quickly but could not have been more pleased with this situation.

With my book on sale a week earlier than expected, I decided to post this new development on social media to bring it to the attention of my friends and twitter followers. By the next day, *The Baseball Gods are Real* was ranked #84 by Amazon on its best sellers' category for baseball biographies and memoirs. It was also ranked #85 on its baseball sub-category of sports and outdoors. Three days later, four days before it should have even been on pre-sale, I was simply amazed to see my book ranked #1 by Amazon for baseball new releases. How was that possible? It was so incredible I just had to wonder if the Baseball Gods were just showing off.

Things became downright surreal when I checked the Amazon rankings for eBooks. Under the category of baseball biographies, my eBook was ranked #1. Ranked #2 was The *Big Fella: Babe Ruth and the World He Created* and ranked #4 was The Life and Times of Ty Cobb. I could not believe my eyes. There was my eBook, with my buddy Jon Perrin on the cover, on the same page with eBook biographies about the great one himself, Babe Ruth, and the legendary Ty Cobb, and my book was ranked above both of them. That was a moment in time I will never forget, no matter how many books I sell in my writing career.

I checked the Amazon rankings again later that day. My book was still ranked #1 but *Maz to Yaz to Amazin': Baseball's Spectacular 1960s*, another new book about baseball, had replaced Babe Ruth in the #2 spot. Since a section of the *Maz* book was devoted to the "Miracle Mets" of 1969, my favorite team when I first started following baseball, I was pleased with the book's rise in the rankings. The miracle—that year the New York Mets beat the heavily favored Baltimore Orioles to win the 1969 World Series.

The next day I googled "*The Baseball Gods are Real*" and discovered that my book was also pre-selling on bookshout. com, another online book retailing website. Here, my book had received a 5-star review. I wondered who had already read my book, even before it was released.

With all this on-line excitement about my book, I decided to drive over to the Barnes & Noble in Leawood to do a little more research. I walked in and faced a "self-help" book display just inside the front door of the store. There were books about self-improvement, self-healing, reiki, mindfulness, essential oils, crystals and even a book on the secret to defeating diabetes. As a spiritual person who practices yoga and meditation on a daily basis, I was pleased to see this display of books chock full of useful information at the forefront. But I was on a mission related to my book and a perusal of these self-help books would have to wait.

I walked up to the information desk and a store manager named Michele asked how she could be of assistance. I told her that I was looking for a copy of *The Baseball Gods are Real*. She typed in the name and, to my surprise, the cover of my book appeared on her computer screen. Michele said that the book was not scheduled to be released until August 28th but it could be ordered now for purchase on pre-sale.

I am sure Michele noticed the surprised look on my face and after I asked her several probing questions about the number of copies on order, shelf space and location, and the book's retail sales price, she started to connect the dots. Michele asked if I was Jonathan A. Fink, the author of the book. Of course, I told her I was. I mentioned that Barnes & Noble had put my book on sale a week earlier than the pre-sale publication date and that I was quite pleased with their decision to do so. In fact, I was thrilled. I joked with Michele that perhaps the Baseball Gods were proud of my book and wanted the world to read it as soon as possible.

On my way out of Barnes and Noble, I stopped at the self-help book display and thumbed through a few of the selections. While I did not spend too much time with the book dealing with diabetes, I have a suspicion that the author strongly recommended exercise, yoga and meditation, along with a strict vegetarian or vegan diet.

I went back to Barnes and Noble four days later and, sure enough, my book was on the shelf in the baseball area of their sports section. Of course, I bought a copy. I walked out of the store with my book in my hand, the credit card receipt in my pocket, and a very big smile on my face. I couldn't help but think, The Baseball Gods are definitely Real!

CHAPTER TWENTY-ONE

The Book Tour

"The noblest art is that of making others happy."
—P.T. Barnum

IN THE MUSIC BUSINESS, A NEW ALBUM BY A ROCK BAND, A rapper or a country group is typically followed by an extensive travel tour to promote its release. Similarly, when a new movie is about to hit theaters, the stars of the film usually appear on talk shows, run a clip from the movie trailer and urge the audience to go out and see it. With the official release of *The Baseball Gods are Real* on August 28th, the Baseball Gods arranged a book signing event for me to promote my book, which I hoped would be the first of many.

Back at Barnes & Noble in Leawood to check on sales, I met again with Michele who suggested I consider a book signing at the store. As a local author, she thought that the event would be good for me and for Barnes & Noble. When I agreed, she told me not to worry about a thing and that she would take care of all the arrangements, including setting the date, ordering a large number of copies of my book, and promoting the event by enlarging my photo in an advertisement in the front of the store.

That night at dinner with my family, after discussing my conversation with Michele and the arrangements for the book signing, I joked that the Baseball Gods would probably schedule a book club event for me next. As if by divine intervention, the next day I received a text from my neighbor, Margie Brown, which read, "I'm reading your book. It is fascinating!! Great job. I picked it up at B & N yesterday and am just about finished. It should be in both the 'Sports' section and 'Spirituality!' Mike is ready to read it next." A few days later, out on a dog walk in the neighborhood, I bumped into another neighbor, Tommy Hanchette. He told me that his wife, Jessica, and Margie were good friends and they ran a book club together. The club had voted the night before to read my book as their next selection and wanted to know if I would be willing to join them for a discussion and Q&A session. I told Tommy that I would be delighted, in fact, honored to do it.

With plans for a book signing and a book club event scheduled, I thought about other promotional activities I could pursue. In the middle of downward-facing dog pose during a hot yoga class, an idea to expand my book exposure came to me. I would contact some of my favorite podcast personalities, send them a signed copy of my book, and, hopefully, convince them to schedule an interview about baseball, spirituality and my path to becoming an author. This idea was well received.

The first podcast interview I was able to schedule was with Wendy Garrett of KCMO Radio and *Conscious Living*. Wendy, a very popular personality with a sizeable following, targeted early November for a live radio and podcast interview on the same day. The second podcast interview I arranged was at *The Positive Head* with Alexa Houser, another popular personality with a solid listening base. My podcast with Alexa would take place shortly after the interview and podcast with Wendy Garrett.

All four of these promotional events went very well. The book club meeting, hosted by Jessica Hanchette, was attended by four women, who brought their husbands. During the Q&A session, the women focused on spirituality, the men on baseball. In addition to family and friends, a few locals attended my book signing at Barnes & Noble and I sold a few copies of my book. My podcast interviews with Wendy Garrett and Alexa Houser went deep into spirituality and discussed yoga, meditation, karma, manifesting, numerology, past life regression therapy and, of course, baseball. All in all, I was very pleased with the content and results of these events.

Even before I participated in these promotions, I was thinking about another marketing idea. I decided to mail copies of my book to local newspapers in an attempt to get editors to assign writers to review it. The first editor I heard from was Barbara Bayer from the *Kansas City Jewish Chronicle*. A few days after our chat, she assigned Steve Hale, a freelance contributing writer, to interview me. Hale's very complimentary article about our interview and my book was published in the Chronicle on November 20th, 2018. The last line of the article was, and I quote, "Not every author has the benefit of the baseball gods looking over his shoulder." I have a framed copy of the article in my office at work and another framed copy is in the home of my amazing 96-year-old grandmother, Doris Koslow, back in New York.

I was still not done with my book launch marketing campaign. During another hot yoga class, the concept of guerilla marketing that I learned about at UMKC business school came back to me. In its simplest form, guerilla marketing is an advertising strategy, popularized by Jay Conrad Levinson in his book with the same name, that promotes products or services locally on the streets and in other publics places. The key component of this low budget strategy is to get the attention of the public and create a buzz about the brand or product being promoted in a cost-efficient manner. These days, guerilla marketing efforts can be much more effective, and can reach virtually thousands of prospects in a short period of time, with the help of social media platforms such as Facebook, Instagram and Twitter.

Putting old fashioned guerilla marketing to work, I went to Kauffman Stadium several times during the last months of the 2018 baseball season and with each visit, I brought four copies of my book with me. My intention was to find serious baseball fans, through casual conversation, who might appreciate receiving a signed copy of my book. Then I would ask if they would mind if I took a photo of them holding the book and posted the photo on the internet. I had little trouble finding willing recipients.

On one visit to the K, the Royals were playing the Baltimore Orioles, the two teams with the worst records in the American League at the time. The game would have no impact in the standings or on the playoffs and, generally speaking, it was a meaningless game. Yet, here were two die-hard Royals fans sitting in the front row in the upper deck behind home plate, both keeping score of the game by hand, with their baseball gloves on, ready and hoping to catch a foul ball. I personally signed books for these two first-rate candidates, took their photo, and posted the photo on the internet when I got home.

Later in the day, I chatted up a lovely couple after I heard the wife tell her husband how much Wade Davis had improved ever since the Royals converted him from a starting pitcher to a closer. I was so impressed with the wife's knowledge of and passion for baseball that I gave that lady a signed book and took her photo. A few innings later, I sat down near a single mother who was with her young son at the game. I listened as she taught him the rules of baseball and during the conversation that followed, I learned that this was her son's first game ever at the ballpark. I signed a book for that woman and hoped that doing so would make this game even more memorable for her and her son.

The next night I returned to the K with four more books. I gave one to the concessionaire that sold me a veggie burger the day before because he was a real baseball fan and he remembered me. Then I ran into Bob Zeldin, my friend Ryan Zeldin's father, who was at the game with his youngest grandson, Jasper, and I signed a book for him. I gave the last two books to the extremely loyal Royal fans known as "King Richard" and "Sign Girl Sam." According to a local news network, these two "super-fans" attend about 90% of the Royals home games and I have seen them every time I have been at the K for a game.

The next time I returned to Kauffman Stadium, I did something a little different. I decided to give copies of my book to employees of the Royals organization. The first lucky recipient was the pleasant woman working in the Royals box office who sold me my ticket to the game. Next, I gave a signed book to a gentleman working security who I had seen at games many times before. I also gave books to the usher who showed me to my seat and lastly, to the friendly baseball fan behind the Customer Service desk.

I truly enjoyed my conversations with all of the folks to whom I gave a copy of my book. Each recipient seemed appreciative of the gesture, happy to receive a free gift, and left with a smile on their face. Traveling circus pioneer P.T. Barnum was surely right when he said, "The noblest art is that of making others happy." For me, I learned that guerilla marketing was not only a useful marketing tool to promote my book, it was also a way for me to meet many new and dedicated Royals baseball fans.

Spending those few days at the K "marketing" my first book to so many Royals fans and employees gave me an idea for inclusion in a future book in my series about baseball. The title probably will be *The Baseball Gods are Real: The Game of Baseball*. A chapter in this book will focus on different careers related to the game of baseball and the interesting people I have met who perform those jobs. Legions of kids grow up dreaming of becoming a professional baseball player for their favorite teams but give up this fantasy long before adulthood, usually after they reach their performance ceiling. Very few ever make it to the major leagues, less than 25,000 in total according to The Encyclopedia of Baseball. However, if you love the game and have retained the passion for it, you should never abandon that passion. Think of that usher working at the K who showed me to my seat. Most likely he has a day job. But at night, he's at the ballpark getting paid to watch the game of baseball, the sport he probably dreamed about playing as a kid.

I got another chance to expand my guerilla marketing strategy weeks later when I took a very early morning flight to Milwaukee, Wisconsin to see the Brewers face off against the Colorado Rockies at Miller Park Stadium in Game 1 of the National League Division Series. I wanted to accomplish several things while in Milwaukee. In addition to continuing guerrilla marketing at Miller Park, I wanted to find out what made Milwaukee such as a great baseball city. I wanted to visit local newspapers and book stores to hype my book and increase circulation. Also, I wanted to continue my research about all things spiritual, esoteric and even paranormal that relate to baseball for volume 3 of my series of books about baseball entitled *The Baseball Gods are Real: The Religion of Baseball*. In this regard, a visit to the famous Pfister Hotel, known as the "Grand Hotel of the West," was on my agenda.

My Baseball Gods adventure in Milwaukee got off to an interesting start right from the Uber pickup location at General Mitchell International Airport. As soon as I got into the car, the driver and I started talking baseball. I told him why I was there and about my new career as an author, writing books on that subject. Then he told me his baseball story. It turns out that he was a former high school baseball star who grew up in Milwaukee dreaming about becoming a professional baseball player and had his own road to the show. He was drafted by the New York Yankees right out of high school and signed a contract with them when he was 18. However, as he explained it to me, in minor league rookie ball he quickly hit his ceiling. As a pitcher, he realized his fastball wasn't fast enough and his curve ball didn't curve sharply enough. As a batter, he was lost at the plate. The pitchers he was facing threw fastballs harder than he had ever seen. When he learned to accelerate his swing and catch up to the fastball, he would face a pitcher with a good curve ball or slider. His road to the show ended very quickly and while he did not say it, I sensed he regretted not having a "plan B," like Jon Perrin and Brent Suter, in case his baseball career didn't work out. When we arrived at my hotel, I gave the Uber driver a signed book and wished him the best of luck.

It was still very early in the morning, too early to visit the many book stores that I had previously mapped out all over the city. My goal was to meet as many of the store managers as time would allow and convince them to stock my book on their shelves. However, with some time to spare, I decided my first stop would be the Pfister Hotel.

Built in 1893, the Pfister is a luxury hotel located in downtown Milwaukee. It is a member of Historic Hotels of America, the official program of the National Trust for Historic Preservation. I learned about the history and splendor of the notorious Pfister while researching material for my first book. At that time, I had cast a wide net of baseball related subjects to consider writing about. I even read *Haunted Baseball* and *Field of Screams*, two baseball books with strange, paranormal themes. These books, and other articles that I read subsequently, described in vivid detail the legendary paranormal tales of ghosts haunting the Pfister. These tales have been told by its guests, including several baseball players. For example, recently the St. Louis Cardinals were in town to play the Brewers. Staying at the Pfister, several players, including starting pitcher Carlos Martinez, claimed that they could not sleep because they felt they were being haunted by ghosts. Martinez even posted his fear on Instagram from his hotel room. The story went viral on social media, the sports press got hold of the story, and the iconic Pfister had another 15 minutes of fame.

I arrived at the Pfister at 8:30 a.m. and the hotel was deadly quiet, no pun intended. I did see several hotel employees standing around like zombies with nothing to do. The hotel had no vacancies and yet, as I walked into the lobby and admired the grand architecture of this vintage building, I realized that not a single guest was walking about. It really felt like I had entered a ghost town.

The Pfister was beautiful. Designed by architect Charles Koch in a Romanesque Revival style, the grand hallway had large chandeliers and I saw wall-to-wall mural paintings on the ceiling, reminiscent of the art one would see in the Sistine Chapel and in many famous museums in Europe. While there, I learned that the hotel houses the largest collection of Victorian art of any hotel in the world. Upstairs, in the second-floor area open to the public, there were displays of antique silverware used by guests at the hotel as far back as 1899. Given its history and elegance, I was sure that the Pfister had hosted many world leaders, dignitaries, entertainers and celebrities as well as ball players who visit Milwaukee and take the field at Miller Park to play baseball against the Brewers.

After my brief tour of the hotel lobby, I decided to speak with a couple of bellhops to illicit some Pfister lore. I had a long, insightful conversation with a gentleman named Shea, the doorman of the hotel. Shea happened to be big baseball fan and, believe it or not, was named after Shea Stadium, the old home of the New York Mets in Queens, NY. He told me that he grew up in Wisconsin but after his mom saw an aerial view of Shea Stadium from an airplane while coming in for a landing at LaGuardia Airport during her first trip to New York, she decided right then and there that if she ever had a son, she would be name him Shea.

Shea was well aware of the Pfister Hotel's reputation for eerie and paranormal occurrences. However, he was quick to point out that in a hotel more than 100 years old like the Pfister, there are a lot of old pipes and floor boards. At midnight, if a guest on the 15th floor flushes the toilet, someone on the 14th floor might think he or she heard a ghost. Just when I was almost convinced that all the legendary hotel ghost stories could be debunked as easily as "old pipes," Shea added, with a serious look on his face, "All that said, if you were to walk the hallways of this hotel's 17th floor at 3 a.m., I guarantee you will feel something."

Shea said the very best story he had ever heard about the Pfister Hotel had nothing to do with ghosts. It was about the New York Yankees. He even retained and showed me a September 29, 1974 *New York Times* article to back up his claim about this crazy story. The Yankees had just completed a four-game sweep of the Cleveland Indians to keep their pennant hopes alive, with only two games left to play against the Brewers. After a three-hour delay at the Cleveland Hopkins International Airport due to inclement weather, the visiting Yankees arrived in town late. The players had been drinking heavily on the short, one-hour flight from Cleveland to Milwaukee, not uncommon back in those days. According to the newspaper article, some players reported that infielder Bill Sudakis and catcher Rick Dempsey had an unpleasant conversation on the flight, which escalated on the bus ride from the Milwaukee airport to the Pfister Hotel. Many of the wobbly, probably drunk Yankees thought this verbal exchange to be just silly banter between two tired, hungover baseball players being baseball players. However, that was not the case and what transpired thereafter was not a laughing matter at all.

While some of the Yankees were already checking in at the front desk, Sudakis and Dempsey began to fight as they got off the team bus. The altercation continued through the front doors of the hotel and into the lobby. Catcher Thurman Munson tried to break up the scuffle but before he could, the fight spilled over into the hotel lounge where many very surprised hotel guests were casually enjoying their after-dinner drinks. The embarrassing story made national news, the Yankees did not win the pennant that year, and the Pfister Hotel enjoyed yet another 15 minutes of fame.

Shea and I had a good laugh about the raucous Yankees lobby fight story. Then, continuing our chat about baseball, he mentioned that the birthplace of the American League was located nearby in downtown Milwaukee. He said that the old hotel where a secret meeting took place to create a new league was gone, replaced by a parking lot, but a plaque in recognition of the event was still there. Before we shook hands and said our goodbyes, I gave Shea a signed copy of my book and took his photo.

With my curiosity piqued and the weather inviting, I decided to take a pleasant walk through the lovely city of Milwaukee and made my way to the birthplace of the American League.

It was easy to find the plaque where the Republican House hotel stood from 1886 to 1961. As the story is told, on the night of March 5, 1900, Milwaukee attorneys Henry Killilea and his brother Matthew, semi-pro baseball players themselves, Connie Mack, who had previously managed the Pittsburgh Pirates, sportswriter Byron Johnson and Charles Comiskey gathered in Room 185 of the hotel. In defiance of the existing National League, Comiskey's Chicago White Stockings (later Sox) were incorporated, and the league's eight team alignment was completed. After the 1900 season, the American League reorganized, placing teams in Baltimore, Boston, Philadelphia and Washington, D.C. and achieved major league status.

As fate would have it, I looked up after reading the plaque and realized that the parking lot I was standing in served the employees of *Milwaukee Journal Sentinel*, the largest newspaper in town. I figured the Baseball Gods had planned this side trip so I decided to walk into the building, introduce myself to the editor, give him a copy of my book, and hope for a review in a future edition of the newspaper. It all happened, except for the review and meeting the editor. As I was leaving the building, I chatted with the friendly security guard at the front desk and I gave her a signed copy of my book.

The Baseball Gods were not done with me yet. I made a right turn out of the *Milwaukee Journal Sentinel* building, then a left turn and walked right past the Milwaukee County Historical Center. Wouldn't you know, the museum just happened to be hosting a temporary exhibit about the history of baseball in Milwaukee. I did a quick loop around this interesting exhibit and got to truly appreciate and confirm what I had previous expected. Milwaukee is a great baseball town.

Much of Milwaukee's sports history can be gleaned by studying the history of Athletic Park, renamed Borchert Field in 1927. Athletic Park was originally built as the home stadium for the minor league Milwaukee Brewers of the Western Association. It was located on a rectangular city block. To make it fit, the layout of the field had short foul lines and a deep center field. The stands were u-shaped so spectators could pretty much see the entire playing field from any seat in the house. Sound familiar? Borchert Field was shaped just like the Polo Grounds.

Athletic Park/Borchert Field in Milwaukee was completely integrated into the neighborhood. This was the case with most stadiums at that time, before the invention of the automobile and the expansion of public transportation in major metropolitan cities. While thousands of ticket holders would sit in the stands to see the games, hundreds of other fans would watch the ballgames from windows, porches, balconies and rooftops of neighboring houses. This is similar to the way people watch ballgames today from building tops adjacent to Chicago's Wrigley Field. In those good old days before the enactment of child labor laws, these stadiums created "employment" opportunities for local children to sell goodies at concessions stands and up and down the aisles of the ballpark. Some kids would retrieve balls hit outside of the park. They were the original ballhawks. There were two taverns near the ballfield and there was a bar in the stadium located behind home plate. This got me thinking about the long-term relationship between baseball and beer.

Later that day, when I had time to do some research, I learned that almost two centuries ago Milwaukee had a large influx of German immigrants who brought with them their know-how for making beer. From 1840 to 1860, more than thirty breweries opened up in Milwaukee. Some of the biggest and most well-known breweries were Best, Blatz, Schlitz and Pabst. Today, the only major brewery remaining in Milwaukee is the Miller Brewing Company, owned by MillerCoors. It is no surprise that the state-of-the-art retractable roof baseball stadium in Milwaukee is named Miller Park.

After what was an already very busy, productive day, I finally arrived at Miller Park to attend Game 1 of the NLDS between the Brewers and the Rockies. I got to the stadium early to check out the pre-game tailgate parties before the gates opened and batting practice began. I walked around the exterior of the stadium to see all of the monuments and plaques honoring the history of baseball in Milwaukee. It was on this leisurely stroll that I discovered the golden age of baseball in Milwaukee, the 13 years between 1953 and 1965.

This period known as "The Miracle in Milwaukee" was essentially a love affair between a team, its players and a community like few others in baseball history. From 1953 to 1965, the Milwaukee Braves, as they were then known, earned their fans' loyalty by consistently playing outstanding baseball, never suffering a losing season. The Braves won two National League pennants, back-to-back in 1957 and 1958, and defeated the New York Yankees 4 games to 3 in the 1957 World Series. In the seasons they didn't win the pennant or World Series, they were competitive and gave their fans something to cheer about every year. Off the field, the Braves became the first National League team to draw more than two million fans in a single season.

The leader of the Milwaukee Braves during "The Miracle in Milwaukee" was Henry Louis "Hank" Aaron, considered by many to be the greatest baseball player of all time. Not to my dad, of course, who thinks Willie Mays was the greatest, Aaron the second best. "Hammerin' Hank," as he would become known later in his illustrious career, began his road to the show in 1952. After a few productive weeks with the Indianapolis Clowns, a barnstorming black baseball team, Aaron was promoted to the Eau Claire Bears of Wisconsin in the Northern League as an infielder. He moved up to the major leagues as a starting right fielder for the Milwaukee Braves in 1954. Leading the Braves to their 1957 World Series victory over the Yankees, Aaron batted .393, hit 3 home runs and drove in 7 runs.

Aaron had a remarkable baseball career, playing for 23 seasons in the major leagues for the Braves, first in Milwaukee and later in Atlanta after the team moved to Georgia. On April 8, 1974, one of the most memorable days in baseball history took place. "Hammerin' Hank" captured the all-time home run record, eclipsing the mark held by the legendary Babe Ruth for decades, with his 715th lifetime home run. A visit to YouTube to hear Vince Scully, perhaps the greatest baseball announcer of all time, call Aaron's momentous home run, is another trip worth taking.

After his 9 seasons in Atlanta with the Braves, Aaron was traded back to the team in the city where "The Miracle" occurred and retired as a Milwaukee Brewer in 1976. His career statistics speak for themselves, 3,771 hits, 2,297 runs batted in and a total of 755 home runs. Aaron was named to an incredible 21 consecutive All-Star teams and was the first player in history to reach both 500 home runs and 3,000 hits. Lastly, Aaron was famous for being a clutch hitter throughout his career, managing to hit pennant-clinching home runs in each of Braves' World Series seasons. He was inducted into the Baseball Hall of Fame in 1982.

When I finished my stroll around Miller Park, I entered the stadium and had a great time at the ballpark. I enjoyed meeting many Brewers fans and chatting with them about their city and their baseball team. I handed out signed copies of my book to folks I thought would enjoy reading it and spread the word. I gave one signed copy to a couple because they loved baseball and had matching Brewers outfits. I gave signed books to two women working at Customer Service because they were die-hard Brewers fans. I gave a husband and wife a signed book because they had taken their son out of school for the game. Maybe I shouldn't have done that. I even met the famous "Marlins Man" Laurence Leavy at the game and gave him a signed book. All in all, it was a great day at Miller Park.

The Brewers defeated the Rockies 3-2 that day in an exciting 10-inning game and went on to sweep them 3-0 to win the NLDS series. Several times during the game, the Brewers fans loudly chanted "Let's go Brewers." Their chanting continued in the aisles and hallways of Miller Park after the game ended and outside all the way into the parking lot. The Brewers were moving on to the National League Championship Series to face the Los Angeles Dodgers, the returning National League champions.

The Brewers/Dodgers match up in the NLCS reminded me of the forecast I had made three months earlier. In July when the Dodgers visited Miller Park to play a series against the

Brewers, I took a screenshot of the game lineups on my iPhone and posted "My prediction for the 2018 NLCS" on Twitter. It was an unlikely prediction at the time because the Brewers were in second place in the standings behind the favored Chicago Cubs and the Dodgers were coming off a horrible start to the season. While this prediction did not come to me during a hot yoga session or a meditation, as many ideas did, I just felt compelled to share my prediction on Twitter, something that I had never done before.

The plan to promote my book identified four key markets to target, Kansas City, Milwaukee, Los Angeles and New York. In Kansas City I did a book club meeting, a book signing, podcast interviews, received a newspaper article review and handed out my book at Kauffman Stadium. In Milwaukee I visited book stores, a newspaper office, a famous hotel, museums and did my thing at Miller Park. Now, with the Brewers heading to Los Angeles for the NLCS, I knew that LA would be my next stop. I immediately booked a flight to the "City of Angels."

The next morning, I googled amazon.com to check on sales. I was pleased to see a solid increase and my book had jumped back into the top 100 in the rankings. To my surprise, my book was listed next to *The Dodgers Encyclopedia*, written by William F. McNeil, and *Sandy Koufax: A Lefty's Legacy*, written by Jane Leavy, two books about the Dodgers. Then I looked more closely at the cover of the book about Koufax and saw the photo of the famous pitcher tipping his baseball cap, as if he was giving me a nod of approval for booking my trip to LA. This was uncanny. Was it a wink form the Baseball Gods? I thought so, and got the message loud and clear.

Initially, I planned to fly to LA to see Game 4 of the NLCS and fly home the next day. However, giving it more thought, I decided that being in Los Angeles would be the perfect time to explore the possibility of making my book into a movie. I reached out to everyone I knew in LA to see if they had talent agent or entertainment attorney contacts in Hollywood. The Baseball Gods got to work and the next thing I knew, I had a meeting booked with an entertainment attorney, thanks to my sports agent friend and fraternity brother, Scott Shapiro. I decided to stay in LA a second night and get a ticket to Game 5 as well.

After a safe, speedy, uneventful flight from Kansas City to LA, I headed straight to Chavez Ravine, the home of the Dodgers, for Game 4. I had more copies of my book with me. I got to the ballpark early to attend batting practice and walk the aisles of the stadium searching for interesting people and baseball fans to talk with. They were not hard to find. A man wearing a Dodgers mascot outfit received a signed copy because of his enthusiasm for his favorite team. He agreed to a photo holding up my book. Then, another Dodger fan received a book because he was here for Game 4 and told me that he was taking his very excited granddaughter to Game 5, passing the Dodgers baseball tradition down to the next generation of his family. Then I gave a book to a woman working the register in the gift shop because she was wearing a Dodgers cap and uniform.

Next, on an escalator on my way to the outfield bleachers, I noticed a woman with a media pass hanging on a chain around her neck. I decided to introduce myself. It turns out she was the director of talent and production for the Dodgers.

We chatted for a few minutes and then I said jokingly, "Hey, if you ever need someone to throw out the first pitch to a game, I'm available." She smiled and said she would keep it in mind. She seemed like a really nice person so I signed a book for her before we said our goodbyes. I also gave a signed book to a Brewers fan sitting all alone in the upper deck late in the game.

The Brewers were in good spirits during pre-game calisthenics and warm up. They were very friendly toward the local Dodgers fans along the railing, joking with them and tossing up plenty of baseballs as souvenirs. During batting practice, I wanted to ballhawk for Nate and catch a NLCS playoff baseball home run that landed in the bleachers. I certainly didn't want to compete with youngsters for balls, so I kept moving around to find an empty spot with no little kids nearby. Just as I slipped into an open area, a towering fly ball came my way. I calmly put out my glove and made the catch. Looking at the ball in my glove, I asked out loud who had hit that batting practice home run. A voice replied, "Ryan Braun."

As soon as I heard that name, I knew that the Baseball Gods were involved. The coincidence was simply too striking for it to be anything else. Recall during Brewers spring training, it was Ryan Braun who spoke with Jon Perrin about investing. This synchronicity had to be a wink from the universe for sure.

Game 4 of the NLCS was a nail-biter. Tied 1-1 at the end of the 9th, the game went into extra innings. During the 12th inning, I received a text from my mother-in-law, Barbara Devinki, asking if I thought Ryan Braun might be related to our family. I replied that he could be because Reggie's grandmother Maria, who had survived the Holocaust, was a Braun before marriage. I texted Barbara that I would check this out after the game, when I got back to my hotel room. The Dodgers scored a run in the bottom of the 13th and won Game 4 by a score of 2 to 1.

That night I googled Ryan Braun. What I learned was both sad and fascinating. Braun's Wikipedia page says that most of his family was murdered during the Holocaust. Braun's father Joe was born in Israel after the war and immigrated to the United States at the age of seven. Braun's mother is Catholic and he did not have a Bar Mitzvah. However, like baseball great Hank Greenberg, Braun identifies as a Jew. Speaking of Greenberg, my research revealed that Braun actually lived for a short time with his maternal grandfather in a house that previously belonged to Greenberg. Quite a baseball coincidence, I would say. Taking the unexpected a step further, Braun is also the Jewish name of Sandy Koufax on his mother's side of the family. I thought to myself, could Reggie, Kayla and Nate be distant relatives of Ryan Braun or Sandy Koufax?

I got a good night's sleep and did yoga and meditation in the morning. Then I set out on my movie quest. The meeting with the entertainment lawyer went very well but I quickly learned that I had a long way to go before I could get Leonardo DiCaprio to play me on screen. The takeaway from the meeting, another successful book or two might help me get a production deal.

After the movie meeting, I headed right back to Dodger Stadium for the early afternoon Game 5. My west coast friend and fellow author Cathy Byrd and her son, Christian Haupt, also attended the game as my guests. We watched Game 5 together from the front row in the right field upper deck on a bright, sunny, perfect day for a ballgame. When I gave Christian the last signed copy of my book, he smiled and seemed to have an angelic look on his face, with sunlight glowing all around him.

The Dodgers went on to win Game 5 by the score of 5-2 in front of 54,000 screaming, happy, loyal fans and took a 3 to 2 lead in the series. Days later they defeated the Brewers in Game 7 to win the NLCS and moved on to play the Boston Red Sox in the World Series. Unfortunately for the Dodger faithful, the Red Sox beat the Dodgers in five games to win it all.

On the flight home to Kansas City from Los Angeles, I had a lot on my mind. First, I missed Reggie and the kids and was anxious to get home for some family time. Second, I had just completed my visit to LA, the 3rd of the four cities I had targeted for guerilla marketing, and was already thinking about a trip to New York to complete the cycle. Third, I was thinking about my next steps toward a Hollywood movie and what I would need to do going forward to manifest that reality. Then I thought about Jon Perrin, his road to the show, and what he would need to do to make it there. Finally, I simply could not get out of my mind the Ryan Braun, Sandy Koufax, Hank Greenberg coincidences. As my jetliner was gliding onto the runway at Kansas City International Airport, it hit me. The Baseball Gods want me to explore these baseball idiosyncrasies in greater detail in my next book, *The Baseball Gods are Real: Volume 3 - The Religion of Baseball.*

THE CONCLUSION

"Relax and Dream"
—Twiddle

IN *THE BASEBALL GODS ARE REAL — VOLUME 2: THE ROAD to the Show*, I took my readers along for the ride as I continued to travel down the road on my spiritual path. Out of the ashes of my midlife crisis, I described how the daily practice of yoga and meditation, and a vegan diet, helped me to find a new, better direction in my life.

This book also chronicled the path of Jon Perrin, my friend and colleague at Satya Investment Management, as he travelled down his road to the show through the Cactus League, the Pacific Coast League and the Texas League, all in one season of baseball.

The Road to the Show introduced my readers to several other interesting baseball personalities and events, some more well-known than others. It showcased the road to the show for a few baseball players Perrin befriended on his baseball journey, including Brent Suter, Jorge Lopez, Aaron Wilkerson, Tim Dillard and Dustin Houle. Additionally, this book featured the road to the show of rookie sensation Shohei Ohtani and told stories about baseball legends Babe Ruth, Willie Mays and Hank Aaron.

I took my readers to cities, airports and major and minor baseball stadiums across the American landscape to share my experiences as an author and as a die-hard baseball fanatic. I hope my readers enjoyed the ride as much as I did.

Finally, as you might have guessed, I used "the road to the show" as a metaphor for the road of life. We are all on the road to "The Show," symbolic for achieving our goals in life, whatever they may be. The road is not flat or straight. There will be twists and turns, ups and downs, successes and disappointments and celebrations and heartaches along the way. But, whether you are an aspiring baseball player, musician, financial advisor or whatever else you might want to become in life, you will learn from every accomplishment and setback, and you will keep moving forward on your own road to the show.

I wish you the best of luck and may The Baseball Gods always be with you!

THE ACKNOWLEDGEMENTS

To Reggie Fink, The Soulmate

To Kayla Fink, The Vegan

To Nate Fink, The All-Star

To Beth and Jeffrey Fink, The Parents and Editors

To Jon Perrin, The Colleague

To Jamie, Brian and Lucy Balanoff, The Planner and the
Pickleball Players

To Doris Koslow, The Grandmother, Chef and
Classical Music Lover

To Sally and Norman Fink, The Grandparents

To Eddie and Janice Fink, The Big Brother and
Sister-in-Law

To Dr. Gary and Aunt Caren Koslow, The 1986
World Series

To Maria and Fred Devinki, The *Guardian* Angels

To Sam Devinki, The Father-in-Law

To Mary Stahl, The Golfer

To Barbara Devinki, The Mother-in-Law

To Jeffery Louis, The Los Angeles Dodgers Fan
To Jennifer Miller and Richard Devinki, The Pilates Instructor and The Producer
To Dayton Moore, The General Manager
To Dean Wright, The Coach
To Dr. Steven and Jordan Rosenberg, The Grapefruit League
To Margie and Mike Brown, Jessica and Tom Hanchette, The Book Club
To Derek Bauer, The Fraternity Brother Mr. D
To Andy Spector, The Running Partner
To Seth Lehman, The Tulane Years
To Seth Kornbluth, The Attorney
To Jeff and Alex Yonteff, The Water Fountains
To Benny Harding, The Money Clip
To Eric Milano, The Roommate
To Paul Greenwood, The Yoga Partner
To Justin and Meg Shaw, The Boston Red Sox Fans
To Bobby Aguilera, The Baseball Prophet
To Scott Shapiro, The Fraternity Brother Sports Agent
To Cathy Byrd and Christian Haupt, The 2018 NLCS
To Aaron Walker, The Police Officer
To Zack Hample, The Ballhawk
To Laurence Leavy, The Marlins Man
To Maryann Maturo, *The Matheny Manifesto*
To Wendy Garrett, The *Conscious Living* Podcast

To Alexa Houser and Brandon Beachum, *The Positive Head* Podcast

To Steve Hale and Barbara Bayer, The Kansas City Jewish Chronical

To Michele at Barnes and Noble, The Book Signing

To Janet Horenstein, The Hostess

To Jeremy McDowell, The Hawaiian Hitfest

To Ian Kennedy, The Vulcan Change Up

To Tim Dillard, The Veteran

To Steve Dillard, The Second Baseman

To Shohei Ohtani, The Rookie

To Dustin Houle, The Canadian Catcher

To Aaron Wilkerson, The Comeback

To Jorge Lopez, The Almost Perfect Game

To Brent Suter, The Raptor

To Brett Phillips, The Autograph

To Lorenzo Cain, The World Series Champion

To Ryan Braun, The Batting Practice Home Run Ball

To Giancarlo Stanton, The Yogi

To Branch Rickey, The Brooklyn Dodgers Visionary

To Willie Mays, The Say Hey Kid

To Jackie Robinson, The First

To Babe Ruth, The Sultan of Swat

To Hank Aaron, The Hammerin' Hank

To Lou Gehrig, The Iron Horse

To Hank Greenberg, The Hebrew Hammer

To David Glass, The Owner
To Clayton Kershaw, Aaron Judge, Ian Kennedy,
Salvador Perez, White Merrifield, Jorge Soler, Lucas Duda,
Robinson Cano and Taylor Williams,
The Fantasy Baseball Team
To Shawn Green, The Author
To Kevin Costner, The Actor
To Prince Fielder, The Vegetarian
To Ben Zobrist, The *SHOW and GO*
To Stephen Kohlscheen, The Investor
To Ty Kelly, The World Baseball Classic
To Sal Biasi, The Trade
To Michael Conforto, The Scooter
To Mauricio Dubon, The Biloxi Shucker
To Colin Kaepernick and Craig Hodges, The Blackball
To Clint Coulter, The Blackjack Player
To Tyler Cravy and Rob Scahill, The 2017 Cactus League
To Joe Carter and Joe Randa, The Kansas City Joes
To Eric Thames, The Meditator
To Pablo Sandoval, The Panda
To Rick Dempsey and Bill Sudakis, The Pfister Hotel
Lobby Fight
To Ted Williams, Carlton Fisk, Bobby Thompson, Sandy
Koufax, Thurman Munson,
Dave Winfield, Don Mattingly, Mookie Wilson,
Lenny Dykstra,

Tommy John, Andy Pettitte, Jim Thome, Derek Jeter,
Doug Glanville, Mike Matheny, Ivan Rodriquez,
Nolan Ryan, Joe Madden, Craig Counsel, Barry Zito,
Alex Rodriguez, Chris Carter, Mike Napoli, Corey Knebel,
Matt Albers, Scooter Gannett, Todd Frazier,
Trevor Bauer, Rajai Davis, Madison Bumgarner, Ned Yost,
Mike Morin, Stephen Vogt, Hideki Matsui, Ichiro Suzuki,
Corbin Burnes, Jacob Nottingham, Brandon Woodruff,
Adrian Houser, Stephen Kohlscheen, Eric Sogard,
Matt Albers, Mike Zagursky, Matt Belisle, Zack Davies,
Mike Moustakas, Danny Duffy, Alex Gordon,
Roman Torres, Kelvin Herrera, Salvador Perez,
White Merrifield, Nick Dini and Carlos Martinez,
The Baseball Players
To the fans and employees of the Kansas City Royals, the
Milwaukee Brewers and the Los Angeles Dodgers,
The Book Tour
To Tom Brady, Wesley Woodyard, David Carter, The
Football Players
To the Kansas City Blaze, The Baseball Club
To Reviewing the Brew, The Fantasy Baseball League
To Forest Green Rovers, The Vegan Football Club
To John Salley, Michael Jordan, Damien Lillard,
Jahlil Okafar, Enes Kanter,
Kyrie Irving, Wilson Chandler, Al Jefferson,
Victor Oladipo, Javale McGee,

Michael Porter Jr., Lebron James and Stef Curry,
The Basketball Players
To Karen and Alan Goldstein, The FG Vacationers
To Bernard Rosenberg, The Rabbi
To Bruce Springsteen, The Promised Land
To Phish, The 'Simple Jam" at Dick's
To Twiddle, The Music Gods are Real
To Iya Terra, The Road to Red Rocks
To The Oak Ridge Boys, The Road to Oak Ridge

2018
Cactus League Opening Day
Milwaukee Brewers v. San Francisco Giants

2018
Cactus League Opening Day
Jon Perrin v. Pablo Sandoval

2018
Brewers Spring training Clubhouse – Maryville, AZ

2018
Grapefruit League
Ballpark of the Palm Beaches – Palm Beach, FL

2018
Coach Wright's Field of Dreams - Raytown, MO

2018
Jon Perrin signing autographs
Security Service Field - Colorado Springs, CO

2018
Derek "Mr. D" Bauer and Jonathan Fink
Kauffman Stadium – Kansas City, MO

2018

Coach Dean Wright, Coach Andrew Reichmeier, and the rest of the U11
Kansas City Blaze (Ian, Tyler, Nick, Nathan, Grey, Drew, Brody,
Brady and Nate)
Overland Park, KS

2018
Jonathan and Kayla Fink

2018

Principal "Field of Dreams" Park – Des Moines, IA
Nate and Jonathan Fink

2018
"Sunset Glow" - *Westport Art Fair – Kansas City, MO*

CPSIA information can be obtained
at www.ICGtesting.com
Printed in the USA
FSHW020706101119
63938FS